Marianne Marsh
with Toni Maguire

Helpless

The true story of a neglected girl betrayed and
exploited by the neighbour she trusted

This is a work of non-fiction. In order to protect privacy, names, identifying characteristics, dialogue and details have been changed or reconstructed.

HarperElement
An Imprint of HarperCollins*Publishers*
77–85 Fulham Palace Road
Hammersmith, London W6 8JB

www.harpercollins.co.uk

and *HarperElement* are trademarks of
HarperCollins*Publishers* Limited

Published by HarperElement 2009

1 3 5 7 9 10 8 6 4 2

© Marianne Marsh and Toni Maguire 2009

The authors assert the moral right to be
identified as the authors of this work

A catalogue record of this book is
available from the British Library

ISBN 978-0-00-728114-5

Printed and bound in Great Britain by
Clays Ltd, St Ives plc

Mixed Sources
Product group from well-managed
forests and other controlled sources
www.fsc.org   Cert no. SW-COC-1806
© 1996 Forest Stewardship Council

FSC is a non-profit international organization established to promote the
responsible management of the world's forests. Products carrying the FSC
label are independently certified to assure consumers that they come
from forests that are managed to meet the social, economic and
ecological needs of present and future generations.

Find out more about HarperCollins and the environment at
www.harpercollins.co.uk/green

Acknowledgements

To my husband, for his encouragement and support in writing the book, but mostly for giving me a life of stability, security, happiness and love.

To my sons also, for their support and understanding, and for completing my life with the happiness they bring me. I am so proud of the men they have become.

To my sister and her family, who have always been there for me, through my rollercoaster life of emotions.

To all of my dear friends, old and new, here and abroad – they will know who they are. Thank you, each and every one of you, for always being there.

To my daughters, thank you for giving me the pleasure of getting to know you and to hold you again.

To Toni, without whom I could not have written my story.

And to Barbara and HarperCollins for making it possible.

Prologue

The man had been looking for a little girl like me even before I was born.

A special little girl, he told me; one who needed love.

He widened his social circle to include young married couples, watched as they became parents and smiled with an inward sly delight when asked to be a godfather.

'He's so good with the young ones,' his friends said.

He married when I was still the baby he had never met and considered his own small daughter for his needs. But his wife had grown to know his soul. She kept her children safe.

Unobserved, he watched me walking down country lanes as I went backwards and forwards to school. Saw my marks of neglect and knew then that I was the one; the one he had been waiting for.

He started frequenting the pub my father drank in and made himself known to him.

Listened to his tale of woe – low wages and small mouths to feed – and recommended him for a job that came with a decent-sized house.

It was no problem, he told my father; a pleasure to help.

People said he was such a fine man, his wife a lucky woman, and how fortunate my parents were to have met him.

He was everyone's friend; the one who remembered wives' birthdays and brought their children presents.

He was the trusted visitor, the favourite uncle.

He always kept sweets in the glove compartment of his car.

I was seven when I first met him, that man; the one who called me his little lady.

Years have passed since he and I last spoke. But still those memories are imprinted on my mind as clearly as though everything that happened happened just yesterday.

Chapter One

'Tell us a story,' my children used to say to me.

'Where do you want me to begin?' I would ask as I picked up a well-thumbed favourite book.

'At the beginning, of course, Mum,' and dutifully I would turn to page one.

'Once upon a time …,' I would start.

But when that story is my own and I have more years behind than in front of me the question is: where should I start?

The tale that I try to keep locked away in the recesses of my mind; that haunts my dreams – that started when I was seven.

My real story, though, started when I was conceived, or maybe even before, but it was not until I sat in my kitchen holding a piece of foolscap paper, with its small neat handwriting covering both sides, that I accepted the time had finally come to confront my past.

But where do I start? I asked myself.

At the beginning, Marianne, my inner voice replied. Your beginning, for you have to remember the years that came before to understand everything that happened.

So that is what I have done.

On every one of my birthdays, during the time I lived at home, before even a card had been opened or a present received, my mother told me how it had rained on the day I was born.

Not just showers, she always said, but great gushes of water that lashed the house and turned the country lanes into muddy paths.

The gutters, which my father never thought to empty of their dead leaves, overflowed. Rainwater streamed down the side of the house and then gushed noisily into already over-burdened drains. Over the years the outside walls had become stained a deep moss green and the blocked gutters had caused large patches of damp and mould to grow on the bedroom walls.

It was the early hours of the morning, before even the farmer's cockerels had welcomed in the day, when I decided to enter the world. My mother had woken to stabbing pains and a damp nightdress and knew I was about to appear. Suddenly she was terrified.

She shook my father awake and he, grumbling at my inconsideration, hastily pulled on his clothes, tucked his trousers into thick boots, placed his bicycle clips over his ankles and rushed out of the house in search of the local midwife.

My mother heard the words 'woman's business' and 'no place for a man' floating in the air behind him before the front door slammed and she was alone with only her pain and fear for company.

In what seemed like hours, but was in fact less than twenty minutes she always eventually admitted, the midwife was standing at the foot of her bed.

A sensible little square of a woman, she quickly took charge and tried to sooth my mother's fears by informing her that she had delivered hundreds of babies. After a hasty examination she confirmed my imminent arrival.

'Then do you know what she said?' my mother would always ask at this point of the story. Obediently I would play the game and shake my head.

'She just said that there was nothing she could do until my pains were closer together, and that,' and my mother would draw breath to put emphasis on her next words, 'all I had to do then was push! And then she asked where the clean towels she had asked to be left out for her were.'

My mother then continued to tell me about the remainder of that long, pain-filled day.

Tutting noises had come from the midwife's mouth when she saw that my hungover father had forgotten to leave out all the items that she had requested, but with my mother's help she eventually found everything she needed.

The next thing she accomplished was bullying a neighbour into agreeing to come next door and help when the time came, but until it did there was little to do. My mother listened to the buzz of conversation downstairs as numerous cups of tea were made and the two of them exchanged gossip. Over the day drinks were brought to her room and her face was wiped with a cool cloth, but mostly she was left alone.

'Call me when you need me,' were the words uttered by the midwife that failed to reassure, far less comfort, before she took herself downstairs to sit before the freshly lit fire.

I sometimes wondered how my mother remembered so much detail, but she assured me she did.

All that day she lay on her back, her legs raised, her knees apart and her hands moist with the perspiration of both agony and fear clutching hold of the twisted sheet. Her bed faced the window and, as she watched the water streaming across the glass, her body was wracked by more pain than she had thought anyone could endure.

Her throat ached with the screams that had been torn from it. She was drenched in sweat; it ran down her face, plastered her hair to her head and dripped from her chin.

More than anything, she wanted someone who loved her there; someone who would hold her hand, wipe her brow and tell her she was going to be all right. But there was only the midwife.

Evening came, and still it rained. She looked out through the window and saw glimmering in its panes her own face's reflection, streaked with raindrops. It was as though, she thought, a million tears were running down her cheeks.

Eighteen hours after I had pierced my mother's waters she gave that final push – the last one she thought her body was capable of – and I finally entered the world.

Luckily as I slid out of the warmth of my mother's body I did not know how much my presence was resented. That took a few years to discover.

My father came home only once last orders had been called and heard the news that I was a girl.

I cannot think that he was very happy.

Chapter Two

My earliest memory comes to me: a time when, too young to walk far, I was sitting in a pushchair. I felt again the motions of its movements and the sudden weight of shopping bags thrown in carelessly on top of me. How I longed for the expected warmth of my mother's arms when she would stoop and lift me out. I heard the buzz of voices coming from the blurred faces above me, saw them peering down at me, but still I could not see myself.

Myself at three, small for my age, with straggly light-brown hair, a pale face that was often far from clean, and round blue eyes that already looked at the world with a cautious and slightly untrusting expression.

I did not know then that I was unloved, for without the joy of being cuddled or the comfort of being tucked up in bed and read to, or the security of being made to feel special, I had nothing to compare it to.

I had no word for fear either, so I could not have explained what I felt when goose bumps crept up my arms, the back of my neck prickled and my stomach felt as though a swarm of butterflies were fluttering around inside. But by the time I took my first shaky steps and formed my first words, I knew it was the sound of my father's raised voice that caused these feelings.

The moment the front door opened and he staggered into the room he would yell at me, 'Who do you think you're staring at?' At first, when I understood the anger but not the words, my mouth would open and release a loud howl that resulted in more shouts from him until my mother crossly removed me from his view. Later I learnt that the moment his presence filled the room I always had to make myself very small and very silent or, preferably, invisible.

The house where I spent my first seven years was a small cottage in a row of six. The front door led straight into our sitting room where narrow stairs led to the two bedrooms. My parents' was just big enough for a double bed and a chest of drawers while mine, with its bare plaster walls and floors covered with brown cracked lino, was hardly bigger than a cupboard. The only furniture in it was a small bed covered with an assortment of old coats and torn bedding pushed against the wall opposite an uncurtained window.

The farm where my father worked as a labourer owned it and, like many farm workers' cottages, our occupancy made up part of his wages.

The farmer, being old fashioned and cantankerous, refused to accept the rising cost of living and paid his discontented workers a pittance. 'They have free housing, don't they?' was his defence. Unfortunately he also believed

that 'free housing' came with no maintenance obligation
for the landowner, and during the winter months it was
a cold damp place. Neither rolled-up newspaper, placed
along the bottom of doors, nor plastic sheeting pinned
to rotten-framed windows stopped chilly drafts nipping
tiny ears and noses and wrapping cold fingers around
bare legs. Shivering, we sought a place by the fire where,
with our fronts warm and our backs cold, we would
huddle round its inadequate small black grate where
damp logs burned.

When the sky darkened and rain sleeted down, making
playing outside impossible, I spent my days in the tiny
living room which served as kitchen, sitting area and, on
the rare occasions when a tin bath made its appearance,
bathroom. Furnished by cast-offs given by both sets
of grandparents, I remember a dull maroon settee with
sagging springs that nearly poked through the threadbare and faded material, a wooden dining table with four
rickety and unmatching upright chairs and a scarred sideboard piled high with saucepans and other kitchen uten-
sils. The living room lacked even one feature that could
have made it either comfortable or welcoming – it was a
dreary, dark room in a dreary, small house.

There were three doors in it: one to the staircase that
led to the bedrooms, one to the back yard, where the
washing of both clothes and dirty pans was done, and the
third, the front door, led, it seemed for my mother, to
nowhere. For apart from going to the shops for our food
and basic supplies, she appeared to have little life outside
of those walls.

Feeding us, which was never an easy task, seemed to take up almost all of my mother's time. My father, even though his contribution to the housekeeping came second to his visits to the pub, expected a warm meal every evening. Regardless of the time he arrived home, should it not be on the table within minutes, his bellows of rage rent the air and meaty fists rose in fury.

He was a binge drinker, as we have now learnt to call them. My mother never knew whether he would go straight to the pub after work or come home first for supper and then head to the pub to drink until his pockets were empty.

Knowing that on the last days before payday he would look for any remaining housekeeping money, my mother tried to hide small amounts so that she could always ensure that there was at least bread and milk in the house. Within hours of her finding a new hiding place for the few coins she had secreted away, my father's desire to drink seemed to give him an uncanny power of detection and he always discovered it.

On those days the tension in the room was almost a palpable force. He'd slurp his tea, shovel his food into his mouth while his eyes darted around the room and my mother, knowing what was to follow, hovered nervously nearby. Maybe she prayed that just this time his mood would lighten and he would choose to stay in.

But he seldom did.

Sometimes he would ask for the money with a smile, other times with a grimace and sometimes with threats but, however he presented it, my mother knew it was a demand and not a request.

Helpless

Her protestations that there was nothing left were always received with an angry glare.

'Sodding liar, that's what you are,' was his normal response. 'Now give it to me if you know what's good for you.'

My little body would shake with fear and I would slither quietly from my chair and creep behind the settee. With hands held over my ears and eyes screwed up tightly, I tried to block out the images and sounds of what was happening. I would hear the scrape of his chair being pushed violently back, the sound of his feet in their heavy working boots stamping across the room, the crash of saucepans thrown to the floor and the clatter of sideboard drawers being emptied onto the floor.

Those sounds mixed with my father's angry shouts of 'Where are you hiding it, you bitch?' and my mother's wasted protests of 'There's nothing left', until the kitchen rang with the sounds of his search and her pleas.

The roars of rage would increase and were followed by the unmistakable thuds of fists connecting with a body. My mother's sobs, the thunder of heavy feet on the wooden stairs and then finally his triumphant shout would let me know that his search had finally yielded its booty.

'There, you useless slag, I said you were hiding it from me.'

Once again the lure of the pub had won. It called out to my father, its siren's call erasing all thoughts of his family's needs.

When the door slammed, announcing his departure, I would remove my hands from my ears, open my eyes, uncurl myself and hesitantly come out from behind the settee. Each time it happened I felt a lump in my throat when I saw my mother sitting slumped in utter despair.

The red marks of a handprint were on her face, a trickle of blood smeared round the edge of her already swelling mouth, a bruise was beginning to stain her arm and the tears of despair were sliding silently down her face as she surveyed the chaos around her. It would make me want to run to her and offer her comfort. There were times when, without the energy left to push me away, she let me nestle against her knee, but mostly, as soon as I said the word 'Mum', she gave me a look of such frustrated anger that I shrank back from her.

'Mum what, Marianne? Can you not leave me alone for one moment? Now what do you want?'

At that age I did not have the words to tell her that I wanted to feel safe, that I wanted to crawl onto her lap and have her arms around me and be told that everything was going to be all right.

Instead, faced with her rejection, fat tears would spurt from my eyes as I wailed with my answering misery.

Anger usually left her face then, to be replaced sometimes by a mixed expression of fleeting guilt and resigned impatience.

'Oh, stop your whingeing now! It's not you he went for, is it? Let's find something to dry your tears.' She would fumble in her pocket for the grubby rag that passed for a hanky and hastily dry my tears. 'You know it's not your fault, Marianne.'

Those brief moments of rough maternal kindness would temporarily console me but I still believed that somehow it must have been my fault that she was angry. After all, there was no one else there to blame.

When there was not enough money left for even the most basic of groceries, my mother had to rely on the good nature of others to give her credit or, worse still, when things were really bad, handouts.

I hated those times when, standing next to her, I heard her stumbling excuses and knew that not only the shop-keeper but the other customers in the queue behind her did not believe her story. I felt a wave of shame as I saw their looks of pity mixed with contempt and wondered if their whispered comments were about us. I watched the blush of embarrassment and shame spreading across my mother's cheeks as she realized she had not been believed.

The cheapest cuts of meat were bought from the butcher. The scrag end of a piece of lamb could last for a week when a bone thick with marrow was added for addi-tional body and flavour. Generous portions of potatoes plus an assortment of whichever vegetables were in season turned it into a nourishing stew that was served night after night.

There was another period, worse than the others, when my father was hardly home. When he finally did appear his face was unshaven, his eyes bloodshot. The smell of the pub, that mixture of alcohol, cigarettes and stale sweat, clung to him, and his pay packet was empty.

It was on these occasions that my mother had to beg the butcher for the meaty bones normally set aside for the well-off customers to give to their dogs. He looked pityingly at her haggard face and at my own pale one. 'Think you deserve these more than pampered Fido and Rover,' he said, also slipping some fatty lumps of meat trimmings cut from his dearer joints into the paper parcel. 'No charge, luv,' he would say and shrug aside her grateful words of thanks. Each time his niceness used to somehow embarrass my mother more than his usual brusqueness would have done.

At these times my mother's stews became even thicker with potatoes and cabbage leaves, but thin with meat. Shepherd's pie became mash and gravy, and greasy white dripping replaced butter and jam on our bread.

'Have to leave the meat for your father,' she would say to me each time she gave me cabbage and chunks of pale potatoes swimming in the grease-topped gravy.

I would just look at my father's empty chair and the place that was laid for him at the table and wonder if he would come home after I was in bed.

Chapter Three

The rows between my parents escalated; cuffs came in my direction too until even the sound of my father's raised voice made me quake with fear. In the mid-fifties there were a number of factories springing up in Essex. They produced a wide range of goods, from Yardley's perfume to Ford cars and tractors, and every time a new plant opened my father's moods would worsen. He bemoaned the way new housing estates had covered once green agricultural fields, putting farm labourers out of work. He sneered at the factory workers and grumbled at the amount of new shiny cars that splattered him with mud as he cycled down the country roads.

His visits to the pub seemed to fuel his anger and he returned back home wound up like a spring. He was a man whose temper simmered just below the surface, ready to boil over at the slightest provocation. Whether it was an imagined slight in the pub, my mother not being understanding enough, or me sitting in a place he wanted for himself, each was enough to send him into a towering rage. And when it did, the power of coherent speech appeared to desert him, leaving only bellows of rage and flailing fists as his means of communication. Flushed and belligerent, his eyes would sweep the room, searching for something to vent his anger on, and I nervously hoped his gaze would not fall on me.

But more often than not I would be curled in a corner trying to make myself as small and invisible as possible.

Although when I hid with my eyes tight shut or lay quaking with fear in my bed, I had heard the screams and shouts and recognized the sound of blows, it was not until I was four that I actually witnessed him hit my mother.

The evening meal had been ready for an hour and she had already put our two portions out when the door crashed open. My father, face flushed with anger, staggered into the kitchen. He leant over the table; his fingers splayed on it for support and the sour smell of his beery breath blasted into our faces as he spewed out his anger, anger that was fuelled by resentment of the better-paid factory workers who had begun to drink in his local pub.

'Those bloody boyos! Who do they think they are? Think they are better than everyone else. They don't know what an honest day's work is. Still wet behind the ears, they are. Bleeding little sods, think they know everything. Do you know what they told me?'

I could sense my mother desperately searching for the right words to calm him down but, not being able to find anything appropriate, she stayed silent.

She just looked at him helplessly, as his angry words spouted from a mouth twisted with rage; words that I had very little understanding of, but I recognized the venom in them and quaked with terror.

'They've put down their names for that new estate that's being built. Going to buy their own houses now. Renting's not good enough for them. Would have thought driving around in those flash cars was enough. They look down their noses at us – us who've worked hard on the farms when they were still at school. Mortgages they're getting, is it? Well, I call it debt. It'll ruin them, see if it don't.'

All the time he ranted about the factory workers his frustration at his lack of achievements kept spilling out. He blamed my mother for trapping him into marriage, blamed me for being there. If, he said, he did not need a job that provided us with a home maybe he too would be driving a new car instead of riding his bicycle.

I pushed myself tighter against the back of the chair as I listened to my mother's murmured conciliatory tones. His dinner was quickly put in front of him, fresh tea was made and poured, a slice of bread cut and buttered, but nothing was going to assuage his fury.

He glared at both of us before picking up his fork and shovelling food into his mouth.

'For God's sake, woman! Can you not cook anything else but this bloody awful stew,' he exclaimed the moment he had tasted the first mouthful. For a moment I thought he was going to throw it onto the floor, something I had seen him do in the past, but some sense of self-preservation, or maybe the knowledge that there was little else to eat, prevented him. Instead he continued to eat, and between mouthfuls he cursed my mother. Then he went quiet.

Judging from the increased colour in his face his temper had not receded; he was just thinking of another reason to blame my mother for his overall dissatisfaction. I could feel both her apprehensive tension and his erupting anger. I felt a knot in my stomach that made me feel sick. I wanted to leave the table but I didn't dare move. I knew better than to draw his attention to me.

He scraped the plate, using a crust of bread to gather up the last drop of gravy. Then with a clatter of cutlery he pushed it to one side and wiped his mouth with the back of his hand. With a venomous look, his eyes raked up and down my mother's body.

'Jesus, what a bloody mess you are. It's no wonder I don't want to come home. You're enough to make a man ashamed. This house's a midden. Think we could ever ask anyone here? My old Ma was right about you: she said you were a dirty cow. She always kept a clean home, and she had four of us to take care of. But you, you lazy bitch, just don't care.'

His face became even more flushed as the insults rained down. My mother cringed as though each word was a physical blow, but she made no attempt to offer a defence.

Suddenly my father's chair was flung back as he rose from the table. My mother must have known what was going to happen next. She tried to retreat but he was too fast for her. She covered her face with her hands as his clenched fists rained blows on her shoulders and her arms. Tears oozed through her fingers, I could hear her soft moans of pain mixed with pleas for him to stop.

Then as suddenly as he had started he stopped and his arms fell to his side.

'Naw, bloody waste of time beating you; you never learn. Look at yourself, woman. Really gone to seed, haven't you?'

His hand rose again this time to poke her in the chest with one meaty finger. 'Look at your damn slip.'

As the derisive words left his mouth my gaze was drawn to my mother's skirt and I saw that her underslip fell several inches lower than it.

A smile suddenly appeared on my father's face, one that scared me as much as his scowl had. He stood so close to my mother that his body forced her to step backwards until her back touched the wall. Fear drained the colour from her face, leaving it a ghostly white. I heard her try and say his name, heard his harsh breathing, saw his hand snake into his pocket and withdraw a cigarette lighter. It only took a few seconds to flick it alight with his thumb. Before my mother had a chance to realize what he was going to do, to my horror he bent down and put the naked flame to the lace hem of her slip. His other hand was pushed against her stomach, stopping her moving.

'Burt,' she screamed, 'please let me go.' She tried to shove him away but he just laughed and held her in place. Panic made me leap from my chair and do what I had seen her do when a spark from the fire had landed on clothing drying in front of the stove. I picked up an old newspaper and, pushing in between them, started beating at the small flame that had taken hold. He sniggered at us and let her go. She rushed to the sink and drenched her skirt with water, and just for a moment I forgot how afraid of him I was.

'You are bad. You are a bad, bad, mean daddy,' I yelled, looking up into his surprised face.

'Who do you think you're shouting at?' he roared back. 'Don't you be cheeking me, you little brat. Get up to your bed now, do you hear?'

His hand cracked against the back of my head and black spots floated in front of my eyes and I nearly fell with shock at the power of that blow. But some sense of dignity made me keep my balance and walk out of that room, up the stairs and into my room.

I kept my tears for when I was alone.

When the rows seemed to continue from one day to the next, my tiny bedroom became my haven.

There I could burrow under my bedding – a mixture of old coats and torn sheets – and pull them over my ears. With eyes tightly shut and my body trembling with fear, I tried to block out the noises that frightened me. Those shouts, screams and blows that I knew came from downstairs or my parents' bedroom and not from my dreams.

But no matter how deep I wriggled under the bedding or how high I tried to pull it over my ears, the bellows of my father's fury always reached me.

'Bitch! Whore!' he would shout, and although I did not understand the words, the ferocity of his rage always made me shudder.

My thumb would creep up into my mouth as my body shook with silent tears and my free hand clutched my rag doll with the painted face. Each time I would also hear my mother's shrill pleas for him to stop followed by her heart-wrenching sobs.

Please make them stop, was the chant that repeated over and over again in my head; but when they did, the thick silence terrified me even more.

But there were days when the blackness of my father's temper lifted. His scowl turned into a smile and he spoke in gentler tones. The trips to the pub, he told my mother, were a thing of the past; he was going to stay in after dinner. She had heard it all before and knew deep down that the period of sobriety would not last, but that did not stop her hoping every time that they would.

On those days, the premature lines that worry had etched onto my mother's face lightened and the basket full of the various materials that made up a rug-making kit would appear. The only sparse flashes of colour in our home came from those homemade rag rugs which, apart from the cold brown lino, provided covering for the floors.

My parents would sit in front of the blazing log fire with the tools, necessary to turn the most basic of material scraps into floor coverings, spread out in front of them. Assortments of threadbare clothing, thrown out for rags by the farmer's wife, a pair of scissors and a pile of sacks were mainly all that was necessary. My mother cut the salvageable material into long strips and sorted it into different colours, then passed it to him to patiently weave into the sacking. Wanting to be useful as well, I silently picked up scraps that had fallen onto the floor and placed them in another bag.

My father would take a long thin piece of metal with a curved hook at one end and a sharp point at the other that resembled a huge crotchet hook, and laboriously thread it with the strips of fabric. His second step was to pull it through what had once been Hessian potato bags from the farm. Then, finally, each fabric strip was knotted into place. My father's calloused hands shook from the absence of drink as he repeated that exercise time after time until colourful rugs of various sizes appeared.

'There's one for your bedroom, Marianne,' he once said gruffly to me when he had finished working on a particularly colourful one. 'Stop your feet freezing when you get out of bed,' and he tossed the completed rug to me.

'Thank you,' I said, grateful not just for the rug but for the unexpected attention. I smiled tentatively at him and received an answering smile back.

That night when I went upstairs I proudly spread the rug beside my bed, and when I woke in the morning I simply gazed down at it, admiring its warm glow. All I wanted then was for his good temper to last, my mother's face to continue smiling and for the angry noises never to start again.

For those were the parents I wanted them to be.

But time after time I was to be disappointed.

Chapter Four

I had heard mention of the word 'school' and knew that it meant I had to sit in a classroom with other children, listen to a teacher and learn how to read and do sums, but until I was told that I was due to start in a week's time I had not paid any attention.

'Marianne, you're not a baby,' my mother said impatiently when I said I wanted to stay home with her, 'so please stop acting like one. Anyhow you'll enjoy it once you get there. You'll make some little friends and it will be good for you.'

But I did not see it that way. Apart from a few visits to my father's relatives, I was not used to mixing with anyone other than my parents. The thought of being away from home made me follow my mother around the house trying to make her change her mind.

'Stop your nonsense, you're going and that is that,' she said when I had repeated my protests for the umpteenth time.

My mother continued to grumble that I knew how busy she was and that I should be grateful that she was going to take and collect me every day, not just put me on a bus. She omitted to say that her reason for taking me on her bicycle was because buses cost money and I was too young to walk the two miles to school alone.

The day I was dreading, my first day at school, came all too quickly. Apart from having my face and hands washed after breakfast it began the same as any other. A dress I had worn several times was pulled over my head, my feet went into black Wellington boots and my hair was given a cursory brush. It was not until a satchel, bought from the second-hand shop, was placed on my back, and I was lifted onto the small seat behind the saddle of my mother's bicycle and told to hang on tightly, that I fully accepted that I was on my way to school.

Feeling every bump of those country lanes, I clung to my mother tightly for that entire journey. Once we arrived at the school she leant her rusty bicycle against the wall and lifted me down. Ignoring the other mothers who stood chatting together in the playground, she walked up to a young woman who, standing with a large notebook in the centre of a group of young children and their mothers, was obviously the teacher in charge.

'Bringing my daughter for her first day,' my mother said abruptly. 'Her name's Marianne.'

'You be good, Marianne – do what your teacher tells you. I'll be here to collect you later,' she said to me before turning and walking briskly to her bicycle. I stared after her, knowing her leaving me was the reason I was feeling completely bereft.

I felt my bottom lip tremble as I saw her peddling away and bit down on it, hoping that my tears would not start. I did not want to look foolish in front of the other children.

'Marianne,' I heard the teacher say, 'come and say hello to Jean. It's her first day too.'

But as I stood in that playground I was overcome with shyness, so instead of doing what the teacher, who I later found out was called Miss Evans, asked I just looked around the play area with the bewilderment of an isolated only child suddenly faced with a sea of other children for the first time.

In total there were around twenty children, all of them showing different emotions. Some had tears in their eyes, others stood in small groups clutching their satchels nervously, whilst their mothers, looking almost as tearful as their offspring, whispered final comforting and encour-aging words before waving goodbye.

But although I saw the tears and the woebegone faces that reflected how I also felt, I was far more aware of how those children looked, and they all looked different from me.

There was not one child dressed as I was. I was very aware of my faded second-hand dress and the cardigan with darns in the elbow – these other children were so clean and shiny they positively gleamed.

Girls' hair was held in place by pastel-coloured ribbons, pretty crisp cotton blouses were tucked into darker pleated skirts and shiny leather shoes covered white-socked feet. Even the boys, with their hair freshly cut in short styles, white shirts with the shop creases still evident, knotted ties, miniature blazers and knee-length short trousers, looked band-box fresh.

I looked down at my own skinny bare legs tucked into Wellington boots, raised a hand to my ribbon-free hair that my mother had cut and which hung jaggedly to just below my ears, and wanted to go home. I knew even as early as that first day that I was not going to like it there and because I was different that I was never going to make friends.

A bell rang loudly and the teacher showed us how to form something she called a crocodile but was really pairs of children forming a queue. We followed her into an airy classroom where we were seated at scaled-down desks. Miss Evans asked each of us in turn to say our names out loud. She told us that we would do that every morning so that she would know if anyone was missing, and as each name was said she ticked a large book that soon I learnt was called a register.

Surely she could tell that just by counting us, I thought, but said nothing.

Next we were each given coloured crayons and sheets of paper and told to draw whatever we wanted. I scribbled lots of wiggly lines, admiring the colours on my sheet.

Half-way through the morning we were given small bottles of milk and a white waxy straw to drink it through.

At dinnertime another crocodile was formed and we were walked to the canteen. As soon as the last mouthful was swallowed we were sent outside to play. That first day I stood on the edges of the playground watching the other children playing. I wanted just one of them to come up to me and ask me my name and invite me to join them; but no one did.

In the afternoon the teacher read us a story. To me it was just words without meaning about things I did not know about. There were no books in our house, just newspapers and the occasional women's magazine, so 'telling a story' was not a concept I understood. Bored, my gaze kept wandering to the window. I saw some of my classmates' mothers drifting into the playground and standing in small groups chattering to one another. My eyes focused on the road behind them – I was waiting for the familiar figure of my mother to appear.

The clamour of the bell announcing the end of the school day rang out and as it trailed into silence I saw my mother push her bicycle through the gates and, exactly as I had done that lunchtime, stand apart from the other mothers. They in turn, like their offspring had done to me, paid her no attention.

'All right, Marianne?' she said when I walked up to her.

'Yes,' I replied, for something told me to say no more.

'That's good, then,' were the only words she spoke before placing me on my seat and peddling away.

She did not ask me any more questions.

Neither did my father.

Maybe they already knew what I was beginning to learn, that children who look different do not make friends.

Chapter Five

It had been many years since I had allowed myself to think of the lonely little girl that I had once been. But as she appeared in my mind, I felt tears prickle at the back of my eyes. I saw her scraggy little form standing day after day at the edge of the playground, hoping, but not believing, that she might make a friend.

I remembered her bewilderment at hearing words like 'holidays', 'central heating', 'conservatories', 'patios' and 'indoor bathrooms', and heard once again shrill mocking laughter ringing out when another child saw her confusion.

I thought of how she had tried to cover up her hurt when as the months rolled by she also heard about birthday parties she was never invited to and presents she could not imagine ever owning: dolls' houses with tiny replicas of modern furniture in every room, three-wheeled bicycles painted a glossy red and dolls whose eyes opened and shut and that cried like real babies.

The children talked of treats she could only dream of: outings to tea shops where pink meringues, scoops of ice cream and fresh raspberries with cream were consumed, of new dresses being bought by doting grandmothers, of trips to the seaside and the funfair and so many other things that set her apart.

Having no stories of her own that she thought she could share, she kept quiet.

I tried to conjure up more images, but my memory seemed fixed on the picture of that little girl standing alone in the playground. Sighing a little, I pushed myself out of my comfortable seat and went to the cupboard where the family albums that recorded happy events were kept. Pushing them to one side I pulled out an old brown envelope that the years had faded to a burnt-out yellow.

Such a thin package, I thought sadly. Although I had not looked at its contents for over two decades I knew that inside it were the only photographs that recorded my first fifteen years. I took those few grainy black and white snapshots out of the envelope and placed them face up on the table.

There were none of me as a gurgling baby or as a toddler clutching hold of my proud parents' hands as I took my first steps. Most of them showed me with other people. It was as though the camera, wanting to capture their images alone, had included mine by accident, for I was always standing on the edges. There were a few school-group photographs taken when I was about twelve. Those I pushed to one side, for I wanted to see myself when I was younger.

There were only two. The first was a black and white snapshot taken of my first brother and me when he was a plump baby and I was a scruffy six-year-old. We were sitting side by side on our old settee. It was me he was leaning against but it was my mother's hand he was grasping. A wide gummy smile was on his face while I, all skinny arms and legs, was gazing blankly into the distance.

That was a time when I had grown to realize that my parents did not love me. Before my brother was born I had not seen my parents bestow tenderness on anyone else, but now when I watched my brother being picked up and looked at with those expressions of care that were never shown to me, I did not doubt it. I had listened to words of endearment being whispered to him and even on one occasion heard my father say 'My boy' with such a note of happy satisfaction ringing in his voice that I felt an emptiness that physically hurt.

For seeing that love, that unknowingly I had yearned for, given to another left a cold empty space under my ribs. I thought then it must be me that was unworthy of it, for my brother had been born too short a time to have earned it. At first when he was just a tiny mewing little creature I would stand looking at him marvelling in the perfection of his rounded limbs and creamy skin, and as he grew so did my love for him – however, with that love came another feeling; not jealousy but more an acute loneliness.

'Look at your little brother,' my mother would say as he took his first faltering steps. 'Look at that smile,' she would say to my father. 'He's going to be a heartbreaker all right.'

I'm over here, I wanted to cry – look at me; but when they did I wished they hadn't, for the fond look bestowed on my brother was absent when their eyes fell on me.

I would watch my mother stroke his rosy cheeks and his neck, and blow kisses on his round little stomach before wrapping her arms around him.

I tried to be good then, offered to help with feeding and changing him, but all the time I asked myself a question repeatedly. If she was capable of feeling so much love for my brother, why wasn't there enough left to give a small slice of it to me?

When our meal was finished I would slide off my chair and pick up the chipped china plates and anything else my small hands could hold. Then, with my brow furrowed in concentration, for I knew not to drop anything, I would take them to the sink.

Sometimes I would be rewarded by a smile from my mother as she ran her fingers through my hair. 'You're a good girl, Marianne, aren't you?' she would say, and on those occasions just those few words of praise were enough to put a smile on my face.

Apart from my brother's existence emphasizing my parents' indifference to me, the biggest change his presence made in my life was that for several months before he was born my mother no longer took me to school. 'Marianne, I'm too busy and you're big enough to go alone now' was all she had said by way of explanation.

So instead of sitting on the seat behind her with my arms wrapped around her body, I had to walk alone for about half a mile to the bus stop and take myself there. That added to my difference, for I was only too aware that I was the only child in my class who walked into the playground alone without a mother to wave goodbye.

And when the final bell rang, I was the only one not collected.

At the end of the school day all the children in my class rushed to the gates to receive hugs and kisses and tender enquiries as to the events of the day. Larger ones held their small hands tightly and they left without even a glance in my direction. I felt as though I was invisible, a feeling that grew when after a few months I arrived home to see my brother sitting on my mother's knee.

Those days I felt an overwhelming need for something in my life, without knowing what it could be.

Chapter Six

It was the second photograph that made me smile. It also had been taken when I was around six, but this time there was an expression of delighted surprise on my face and I clearly remembered the day when the button on the camera was pressed, capturing that moment for ever.

I knew that my father's family had no affection for my mother and very little for me. On the rare times they called on us I had seen the expressions on their faces as their eyes slid around the dirty room before alighting on me.

'She takes after you in looks,' my grandmother always said to my mother and I understood it was not meant as a compliment. So what my father did was surprising.

He was the eldest of four children and, despite his forced marriage to a woman his family disapproved of, was still his mother's favourite. His father had died while I was still a toddler, so when his sister announced that she was getting married she asked my father to give her away.

He in turn asked two things of her. His wife was to be invited to the wedding, and I was to be bridesmaid.

Neither my mother nor I was present when he made his request. All I knew was that my aunt had said yes and that I had been taken to my grandmother's house to be measured for my dress.

If it is love that makes a child pretty and parental affection that puts a bloom in small children's cheeks, then my lack of either explained why I was an unprepossessing pale-faced child; one dressed in badly fitting cast-offs from charity shops and one who seldom saw the inside of the tin bath. The expressions on both of my aunts' faces left me in no doubt of their opinion of me.

'Going to take more than a few minutes to get her ready,' the elder one had said, after taking one look at me.

'Bring her over the evening before so we can tidy her up. She's such a little scrap we can put her in my bed to sleep – sure I won't even notice her there.'

So the evening before the wedding I was dutifully delivered into the care of my aunts. A beautiful pink silk dress was laid out on my aunt's bed, ready for me to wear the next day.

'Bath! ' said my aunt after I had eaten my supper.

'Here,' she said to her sister, 'help me out will you? I've still things to do for my big day.'

My hand was taken and the next thing I knew my clothes were on the back of a chair and I was looking at a huge white bath filled with bubbles. 'In you get,' said the younger aunt, not unkindly.

For a second I was scared. It was so big, surely I would drown in it? But my aunt's strong adult arms held me tightly as she lifted me in. Soap was lathered over my face, neck and body, shampoo rubbed into my hair, and then with instructions to close my eyes she tipped me backwards. My head went under, my legs kicked out; soap was in my mouth, laughter in my ears. Choking, they raised me to the surface.

'This time keep your mouth shut as well as your eyes,' they warned me, then under I went again.

'Blimey! Grubby little mare our niece is!' said a voice I recognized as belonging to my younger aunt. 'Wonder when she was last as clean as this?'

'You could have flaked bits of grime off with your fingernails,' I heard the older one say to her sister. 'Whatever is that mother thinking of?'

'Good thing she ain't got nits, or you could count me out doing the pinning of her hair later.'

It was me they were talking about. And knowing the shame of it, it the happiness and excitement of the day faded. Suddenly the arms that held me close now constricted me. The friendly laughter had become mockery and the comments had turned into criticism. I wriggled in protest.

'Oh, come on love, don't you get narky,' said my aunt when she saw my discomfort. 'Sure we're all girls together tonight, aren't we?'

'Course we are,' they both said in unison, and suddenly I was lifted up onto a knee, a fluffy white towel was wrapped around me and my aunts' arms hugged and petted me. A sweet was popped into my mouth, my hair was given another quick rub, the tangles carefully combed out, then, while still wet, coils of my light-brown hair were wrapped in rags and pinned tightly to my head.

'Don't spoil it now, Marianne,' the elder aunt said. 'You are going to be so pretty tomorrow with your hair all done up.'

'Yes,' said the other one, 'a special little girl, that's what you'll be.'

'You sleep with your neck on the pillow as well your head,' said her sister helpfully. 'Don't want to lose these rags.' And with all the excitement I hardly noticed any discomfort as I tried to quell the excitement and sleep. The last thoughts as I finally fell into a deep sleep were 'Tomorrow I'm going to wear a beautiful new dress and I'm going to be special.'

The next morning, in a bedroom where the older bridesmaids were fluttering around mirrors and jostling to gain a better view of themselves, my younger aunt took the rags out of my hair, brushed it gently, then pinned it up into a soft roll. Next, new pink underwear was pulled on, white socks went onto my feet that were then slipped into shiny black shoes. I could hardly keep still for excitement when finally my wonderful new dress was pulled over my shoulders.

'Close your eyes, Marianne.' I squeezed them shut, felt my hair being smoothed back into place. Hands gently took my shoulders and turned me around to face a large mirror.

'Look, Marianne, look how pretty you are!'

Out of the glass a child I hardly recognized stared gravely back at me. As our eyes met a look of astonished delight spread across her face and I, feeling that joy, felt my mouth stretch into an answering wide smile. That was when they took the photograph.

The wedding might have been the most important day in the bride's life, but I felt it was mine as well. Every mirror I passed was stopped at for me to admire my reflection. At the end of the day I went home still wearing my new clothes.

'They are for you to keep,' my younger aunt told me when I thought they must be returned. And I beamed at her with happiness.

She bent down and gave me a kiss, and as I inhaled a mixture of soap and perfume, I knew then what it was that I so wanted. For twenty-four hours it was as though a curtain separating our two worlds had been pulled back, allowing me to step into her world. I wanted to be part of it – a world where houses were full of laughter, children wore nice clothes and little girls were told they were pretty. I wanted to feel special again. It was to be another year before I felt that – it was when I met the man who called me his little lady.

Chapter Seven

When I look back on my parents' marriage I think it had taken those five and a half years of my being an only child for my father to come to terms with no longer being single; certainly matrimony was not a state he appeared to enjoy. I learnt as I grew older that my parents' marriage had been a rushed event, with me being born less than five months after the ceremony. When his eyes fell on me he seemed to remember that I was the cause of all his unwanted responsibilities. His brows would lower, thunderous looks were cast in my direction and at a very young age I quickly learnt to keep out of his way.

When the first of my siblings arrived, a boy, the birth of a son appeared to please my father more than my presence ever had. The tiny red-faced scrap was leant over, smiled at and even on some occasions spoken to. For a brief interlude my mother also appeared content, but no sooner was my little brother crawling than she announced that another baby was on the way.

Maybe the imminent arrival of another mouth to feed made him seek fresh employment, or perhaps with his surly manners and quick temper he had upset his employer. Whichever it was, my father took work on another farm, one where the wages were higher and the rent-free cottage larger.

'Got a new job,' he had announced at the supper table and named the farm that would be employing him.

'We'll be moving too, so you can start packing,' was all he said about it.

My mother only asked him where the cottage that was going to be our new home was.

The woman my mother had been, before I came along, might have questioned him more, but seven years of marriage had taken their toll. She showed very little interest in herself and far less in what was happening around her.

Her husband's drinking and frequent violence, the greyness of poverty, and her total lack of independence, for my father controlled what little money there was, had slowly stripped away nearly all her youth and confidence.

I was surprised that over the days leading up to our moving my mother suddenly appeared happy, put an effort into the evening meal and smiled at my father. She told us both that she had taken herself for a walk to inspect our new home, which was nicer than she had expected, and met our new neighbours.

It was clearly the last part that had put the smile on her face.

'The people next door seem very nice,' she had said as she placed my father's dinner of stew and potatoes in front of him. His response was to lift his fork and commence eating.

'Yes, they do, really nice,' she continued. But her words vanished into the silence of disinterest.

Maybe it was then that I recognized the loneliness that my mother endured on an almost daily basis. For hours at a time she was alone in the house with just a brown Bakelite radio for company, and she longed for another adult to talk to. That evening I heard that barely concealed flicker of hope in her voice – hope that she might make a new friend and be able have a conversation with someone other than herself, her small children or her morose husband.

Two weeks later, when we moved to our new home, it seemed that my mother's wish was to be granted.

Chapter Eight

The week before we left the tiny cottage that my mother disliked so much, I helped her pack up our meagre possessions. Bits of kitchenware poked out of cardboard boxes, bedding bulged out of stained pillowcases and clothes had been crammed into two battered second-hand suitcases.

I refused to put either my collection of rag dolls or my beloved blonde-haired favourite into a box. She had been a present from my aunt and I had named her Belinda. Instead I wrapped each one up carefully in whatever scraps of material I could find and placed them in a brown carrier bag that I refused to be parted from.

Two vehicles, a maroon car that had seen better days and an equally battered white van, both driven by my father's friends, arrived on the morning of our departure. My mother, my small brother and myself, still clutching my precious bag of dolls, were placed in the car, whilst my father and our ragged assortment of possessions went into the van.

Sitting in the back of the car I wondered what our new home would look like. My mother had told me that a young couple with two small children lived in the adjoining cottage. A boy and a girl, she said, but to my disappointment they were still only toddlers, so too young for me to play with.

The husband was a mechanic. He serviced all the farm's vehicles and that was why the farmer allowed him to rent a cottage on his land. She had only seen him briefly, but his wife was very friendly.

As my mother chattered away about our new neighbours with more animation than I ever remembered hearing in her voice, I looked out curiously at the flat scenery of Essex flashing past. First, there were large farmhouses with pretty gardens and then clusters of farm workers' cottages with unkempt gardens and broken wooden fences. Then we drove down a long country lane where clumps of flowers added colour to the hedgerows and cows grazed peacefully in the fields on either side. Just as I was craning my neck to see more, the car slowed down and we knew we were there.

In what looked to me more like a large field than a garden stood two red-bricked cottages with fresh paint-work on the doors and windows and a sweep of gravel in the front, large enough for the two cars to park.

My eyes were drawn to the cottage next door. There were pots of geraniums on the front step, pale curtains hung in the windows, wisps of smoke curled out of their chimney and on their lawn a sturdy swing had been erected.

When my father pushed open the door of our cottage it smelt fresh and welcoming. A shiny black stove was at the end of the stone-floored living room. Flowers patterned the newly papered walls, and when we walked through to the kitchen I saw a sparkling white sink.

My father and his friends started unloading the van, and within minutes, it seemed, it was empty. The beds had been carried upstairs and the rest of our possessions were piled in a heap in the centre of the room and finally my father's bicycle was removed and propped up against the outside wall.

My brother, tired and grizzling, had been placed in the pram and thankfully had shut his eyes and fallen asleep.

'Anyone for a cuppa?' my mother asked brightly.

'Thanks love, another time. We had better be off,' the men said without any further offer of help, and we watched from the doorway as the van and car drove off up the lane.

'Done all I need to,' said my father. 'I'll just go down the pub and buy those two a couple of beers for their help. They want to introduce me to a few of the regulars, now that it's going to be my new local. Marianne's old enough to help you now. Anyhow, arranging furniture and stuff is women's work.'

Before my mother had a chance to protest he mounted his bicycle and pedalled off in the same direction his friends had taken.

I put down my bag of dolls carefully and glanced up at my mother who was just staring dolefully at my father's retreating back.

Her shoulders slumped despondently as she gave a sigh at the thought of how much had to be done with only a seven-year-old to help. All the animation and expectation drained from her face, leaving her looking worn out and defeated.

'God,' she said to me, 'where do we start?' while I, having no answer, just stared helplessly around the room. 'I'll help, Mum,' I said without much idea how I was going to achieve that.

No sooner had those words left my mouth then I heard a crunch of gravel and saw a smile forming on my mother's face. A voice called out 'Hallo there' and I looked up to see a tall blonde woman with hair swept up in a fancy hairstyle and her feet strangely, considering we were two miles from the village, wedged into fashionable high-heeled shoes.

She bent down to my height so that our eyes met and smiled. 'Hallo,' she said. 'I'm Dora. I live next door,' she added unnecessary, as ours were the only two cottages in that part of the lane. 'You must be Marianne,' and I smiled back at her and nodded furiously.

'I know what it's like on a day like this,' she said to my mother, making no reference to the fact that we had been left without any help. She just gave her a small pat on her shoulder and said lightly, 'Expect you could do with a break before you start. Come round to mine – the stove's lit and I've got a brew all ready.'

My mother, giving a rueful look at the boxes and bags strewn around the floor, accepted gratefully. I wheeled the pram and followed them over the short distance to the other front door that, like ours, led straight into the living room.

A large wooden playpen dominated nearly two-thirds of her space. Inside it her two toddlers were playing contentedly with brightly coloured wooden building bricks. More toys were scattered within throwing distance on the floor outside it.

'My most useful bit of furniture!' she remarked laughingly.

'Come here, little man,' she said to my baby brother, who had woken and looked ready to let out a shriek. She quickly scooped him up and, before he was able to voice his protest, swung him in the air, making him giggle loudly. Then she swiftly plopped him down in the pen beside her two. A wooden car was passed to him and tears were forgotten as his plump little hands stretched out and grasped it. We were all rewarded by a wide gummy smile before he turned his rapt attention to his new toy.

'There, that will keep him quiet,' she said matter-of-factly and gestured to my mother to take a seat.

A plate piled high with individually iced cakes suddenly appeared and was placed on the table in front of me.

'Help yourself,' the neighbour's wife said with some amusement when she noticed I could hardly tear my eyes away from it. Needing no more encouragement, I stretched my arm out and chose a pale-pink iced one, which was decorated with tiny silver balls. Biscuits and juice were given to the three little ones and cups of hot sweet tea were poured for my mother and me.

For the first time that day I saw my mother relax. An hour passed quickly while the two women chatted to each other. The three younger children, bribed with further biscuits, played happily and I amused myself by surreptitiously helping myself to more cakes and looking at the pictures in a women's magazine. Treats such as these seldom appeared in our house.

'Leave the baby with me,' Dora said as we reluctantly started to take our leave. 'It will be a lot easier to tackle that unpacking if you haven't got him under your feet.'

This was an offer my mother readily agreed to.

Already the bond of a new and longed-for friendship was forming.

Chapter Nine

A week after we had moved in my mother invited Dora to tea.

'Don't know what you women find to talk about,' my father said grumpily, 'especially as you see each other every day. Well, I'm off to the pub after work. Be back for my supper.'

And with those parting words he left and I saw a look of relief cross my mother's face.

That day she sang a happy tune under her breath. I think she thought then that maybe there was going to be a life for her outside of her own four walls. I imagine that she dreamed of shopping together with her new friend, maybe some afternoons at the cinema, perhaps having coffee together in the morning. Perhaps just for that day she did not allow the sharp prick of reality to pierce that dream by allowing herself to remember her complete lack of money.

That warm spring afternoon I was sent outside to play. My baby brother was confined in an improvised version of a playpen, made out of boxes and a fireguard, and my mother clearly did not want me under her feet either.

She had made me wash my face and hands earlier, then put me into a clean dress that she had found that week in a second-hand clothing shop.

'We have visitors coming,' she told me unnecessarily. 'You are not to wander off and you are not to get dirty,' and I obeyed, for the aroma swirling out of the stove of gingerbread men baking was making my mouth water and I knew that if I disobeyed there would be none for me.

The old sheepdog, visiting us from the farm, was dozing by the back door. Flies flew round his head and one settled on his nose but although his body twitched he refused to wake. The few hens, which provided us with daily eggs, clucked as they scratched the gravel, their beady eyes searching the ground for food.

I sat very quietly on a small stool enjoying the warmth of the sunlight and watching a fledging taking its first lesson as it learnt to fly. I had discovered the nest the day after we had moved in. Hearing some rustling, I had peeped into the hedge and seen the cluster of woven twigs with the baby birds nestled inside their nest. Carefully I replaced the leaves that protected it from sight and later saw the mother bird returning with morsels to feed her young. Every day after that I sat and watched the small feathered family, hoping I would be there for precisely this event.

That day, as I watched the tiny birds ruffling their feathers in the warm air I was so intent on sitting as still as possible, so as not to startle them, that I was completely oblivious to the pair of gleaming eyes fixed on its prey, nor did I catch sight of a tongue that licked its lips in anticipation and a bottom lip that trembled with the excitement of a kill. I was completely oblivious of the danger slowly creeping towards us.

I felt no sense of warning nor did I hear the slightest sound as with slow careful steps the predator tiptoed closer. I was only aware of it when it pounced and I felt a faint breath of air on my skin.

A shrill squawk abruptly cut off rose into the air, feathers dipped in blood floated in front of my horrified eyes and I screamed. The farmer's cat, a pale bloodstained feather still clinging to its mouth, its fur bristling with bloodlust, arched his back and glared back at me. There was no sign then of the family pet, or the soft purring creature I so loved to stroke. The cat showed no remorse as he turned and slunk into the bushes carrying a fledging in his mouth.

The mother bird lay in the dirt, a mess of bloody feathers. One eye seemed to look straight at me with what I thought was reproach before slowly glazing over. I screamed again.

My mother came running to where I stood howling. Snot ran from my nose, tears leaked from my eyes and streamed down my cheeks. With a shaking hand I pointed to the pathetic corpse. 'Look, look what the cat did,' I sobbed loudly.

'Come Marianne, stop your noise now and come in to the house,' my mother said and took me by the arm. I jerked it back angrily. It was then that a car drove into our communal yard. Through my tears I saw a slim, dark-haired man alight and come towards us.

'There, there,' were the first words I heard him say. 'Why's a pretty girl like you crying?' And I, unused to kind words, looked up into his face for the first time. I saw warm brown eyes seemingly full of concern for my distress looking back at me. He smiled at my mother, then held his hand out.

'Come,' he said, 'I have something that will make you feel better,' and I unquestioningly slipped my small one into his. He pulled me gently to my feet and drew me over to his large black car.

Opening the door he took out a bag of brightly coloured dolly mixture sweets from his glove compartment and tipped a small mound into my hand.

'I just knew they would be your favourite,' he said. And I, with the instant trust that only a child can feel, gazed up at him. 'How had he known that?' I asked myself. 'How did he know when he has never seen me before?' The picture of the dead bird started fading from my mind and, with my free hand tucked into his, I followed him into my mother's kitchen.

He sat on our settee and I, with a need to be near him, perched on its arm.

'It's what cats do, Marianne,' he told me softly and wiped the last streaks of my tears away gently with a clean white handkerchief. 'They find what's weak and kill it. But it's part of their nature and we can never change that, can we? No, we can never change our nature.'

And I, still far too young to understand, just nodded.

He put his arm lightly across my shoulders, drew me closer and whispered softly to me, 'There's my good little lady.'

Chapter Ten

I shivered as those memories came back.

I thought of the care I had taken over my children as they grew. I had never been able to become a parent content just to warn her children not to speak to strangers. Instead every one of my husband's friends was examined with suspicion, each male neighbour viewed with caution, and should a friendly hand move to touch the head of one of my sons, while a male voice murmured the comment of 'What a fine boy you have there,' my body would stiffen with something approaching revulsion.

Invitations for my sons to visit their friends' houses were inspected carefully, questions as to whether both parents would be there frequently asked.

'Don't make such a fuss, Mum,' said my sons with some irritation when faced with my vigilance. 'We know not to take sweets from strangers!'

Then I would remember the vulnerable little girl I had once been and the man who had sought out a needy child and how he had gained her trust before controlling her by fear.

For how could I explain to my sons that it was not strangers I was scared of?

Our new home was further away from my school. It took me nearly an hour to walk to the bus stop, but I did not really mind. I liked where we lived, liked the fact it was clean and that my mother seemed happier. Even my father appeared more content.

It was spring when we moved, and for the first few weeks the sun shone. I could smell the promise of summer in the air, and summer meant long weeks of holidays and freedom from school. But when the treacherous English sun disappeared behind dark clouds and squally winds blew across the fields, bending the trees and scattering their leaves, the lanes seemed to grow longer and my home too far away. It was then that I shivered from both the cold and a tiny kernel of apprehension.

It was on one of those blustery days when rain trickled down the back of my neck, my Wellington boots chafed damp bare legs and my satchel grew heavier with every step I took, that I heard the sound of a car slowing down behind me.

As I stood on the verge waiting for it to pass I heard the sound of the engine slowing as the car came to a stop, and with an inherent fear I was suddenly aware of how dark it had become and how far away the nearest house was.

'Can't have my little lady getting wet now, can we?'

For a second I froze. Although the reasons had never been made clear to me I had been told never to talk to strangers.

'Just do as I say and don't ask so many questions,' my mother had snapped when I had asked her why.

But this was a voice I recognized: it was the man from next door.

'Come on, jump in.' And needing no persuasion to get out of the rain I swiftly obeyed.

A small towel appeared; my hair was quickly rubbed and gently tousled back into place. My hands, reddened by cold, were taken in his larger warm ones. 'Soon have you warm as toast,' he said, blowing on them before gently rubbing my fingers.

Opening his glove compartment, he reached in and drew out a yellow tube of sherbet with its black liquorice stick. 'Here, this is for you. A little bird told me you liked them as well as those dolly mixtures,' he said with a wink.

Licking my sherbet delight I sank back contently on the leather seat. This time when I arrived home the journey had been too quick.

The following day when black clouds promised more rain he was waiting by the school gates.

I saw the other children look at his car and suddenly felt my chest swell with pride. Not only had someone met me, but someone with a big black car.

'Can't have her getting her death of cold,' he said to my mother as he walked me into the house.

'That's kind of you,' she said, before turning to me. 'Say thank you, Marianne,' and I did.

Now every day I wanted it to rain because if it did I was sure he would be waiting.

Chapter Eleven

By the time I reached seven I knew that it was not nice to be dirty. At school I was told to wash my neck, remove the dirt out from under my nails and brush my hair. I tried to scrub myself clean but the mirror that my father used for shaving was too high for me to see into. I knew my clothes were not washed often enough and that my hair was greasy. It was Dora who helped me then.

'Your mother's so busy with the little ones,' was all she said when I complained that the tin bath rarely made an appearance and I was getting into trouble at school. 'You can bath here.'

And once a week that is what I did. She gave me nice-smelling soap and talcum powder, and when I told her I hated changing for PE because my knickers were so grey she bought me new underwear.

'It's just a present,' she told my mother when she protested. 'She's so good at helping with the children that I owe her something.'

I loved the feeling of being clean all over and liked the fact that my skin smelt of flowers. Dora showed me how to put my hair into rags. 'Just brush it out in the morning,' she told me, 'and you will look a different little girl.'

So each morning after that I went to school with curly hair, a face scrubbed clean and a hopeful smile that someone there would like me now. The teachers stopped complaining about my grubby appearance, but the children still saw my faded second-hand clothes and Wellington boots; they continued to ignore me.

The Easter holidays came and my sister was born, and once again I saw my parents showering another member of the family with love. This time my mother's energy seemed sapped by the demands of a new baby. It seemed that nearly every time she spoke to me it was to ask me to do something for her.

There were rare occasions treasured by me when my mother seemed less tired, and then she would smile and run her fingers through my hair. 'You're a good girl, Marianne, aren't you?' and just that tiny slice of praise was enough to put a smile on my face.

But mostly after I helped as much as I could she barely paused in what she was doing to mutter thanks.

More and more it fell onto me to baby-sit my brother who had reached the age when fingers went in electrical sockets and the contents of unlocked cupboards were scattered onto the floor and put into his waiting mouth.

'Bring him round to play with mine,' Dora told me when she saw me watching the pram.

'You're such a little mother,' Dora would tell me as I sat by the playpen watching my baby brother and her two playing happily together.

I would beam at her praise, drink the orange squash she gave me and eat the shop-bought biscuits, but all the time I listened for *his* footsteps, willing *him* to arrive before I left.

Suddenly the neighbours were the parents I would have liked to have. But for all Dora's kindness to me it was *he* who in my imagination became the father figure I could turn to, and I became a daddy's girl who followed him around like a small puppy that had only just found someone to give it attention.

It was he who always had time to answer my little girl questions.

'Why are there no mice in the skirting boards? Where have they gone? Mum says they will be back soon enough.'

'Well, little lady,' he would answer patiently, 'in winter when it's very cold they can't find food so they creep into our homes and hide. When we are in bed asleep they run around looking for crumbs. But before we wake up they hide themselves away again.'

'In the skirting boards?' and I imagined the families of mice peeping through the holes just waiting for us to go to bed so they could have their midnight feast.

'Yes, in the skirting boards,' he would reply, laughing at my inquisitiveness.

'Why does my mum get angry when she sees them?'

'Women don't like them' was his only answer to that.

Other times he would make shadow pictures of rabbits, dogs and even a horse on his walls. Then when I begged for more he took off his brightly coloured neckerchief which, apart from Sundays when it was exchanged for a tie, he always wore knotted around his neck. Once off he somehow twisted it so that it cast shadows of birds against the wall.

Peter and Paul, he called them, as they flew up and down the walls. And before they disappeared out of sight a wing would gently caress my cheek. Those days I smiled happily back at him as I felt a glow spread through me at his attentions.

From my bedroom window I could see the man next door's workshop. Sometimes he had a car he was repairing sitting outside it. I would wait for him to appear, then clatter down the stairs.

'Shall I take Stevie out, Mum?' I would ask, pointing to my brother.

'Yes, you do that, Marianne. Keep him from getting under my feet,' was her standard reply, so grabbing the toddler's podgy little hand I would take him into the garden and wait hopefully to be noticed.

I never had to wait long. As though he could sense my presence his head would turn in my direction and a wide smile would light up his face.

'Marianne,' he would call, 'come and give me a hand with this car, will you?' and, delighted to feel needed, I would drag my unprotesting brother along as I flew to his side where I would importantly hold a spanner, pass a tool or even help polish the chrome.

Luckily my little brother was a sunny-natured child whose good behaviour could be bought with a biscuit or sweet.

'Give the back seat a good wipe, will you, Marianne?' he would often ask and, intent on my task, I would obediently crawl over the front seat.

'Good girl,' he would breathe in my ear as his hand patted my bottom.

'You've got a little marvel there,' he told my mother each time she appeared to see what I was up to. Ignoring the fact that he had taken up time when I could have been helping her, she gave him an answering smile.

'Yes, she's always been a good child, has Marianne. Never given me any trouble.' And her naive complicity in his attentions was what sealed my fate. Maybe a worldlier woman might have questioned his motives. But he was our neighbour, the one who had helped my father find his job, while Dora had given my mother something she had craved: friendship, and with it the end of lonely days. So if there were any beginnings of doubts my mother did as so many mothers have before her and will do in the future: she doused them firmly down.

And finally I had someone in my life who thought I was special. He told me I was pretty, gave me sweets and endlessly listened to my chatter, and that was all it took to capture my seven-year-old heart.

Chapter Twelve

The tiniest thing can often change the course of our lives, and mine was changed the day the little white cat found her way to our house. It was after that that the fear I felt of my father turned to mistrust and my love for my mother faltered as I saw her weakness.

I had reached that age when I wanted a pet of my own; something I could hold and cuddle, something that I could look after, take into my bedroom for company and tell my childhood fears to. Somehow my doll was no longer enough.

'No,' my mother said when, with all memory of the one that had killed the bird forgotten, I asked her for a kitten. I knew better than to ask my father. There might have been a whole colony of cats at the farm where he worked but they were only tolerated because they kept the population of rats and mice at bay. But still I looked wistfully at them. It was them, not the big black and white dogs who jumped up and frightened me, that I wanted as my friends, even though they seemed to view the human world with lofty disdain.

I first saw the little white cat when my mother and I had gone to the farm to buy fresh eggs. She was sitting in the shadows of the farmyard fastidiously cleaning her fur. My eyes met her bright-green ones and I knew she was not the same as the feral cats that lived there. I went to her side and gently stroked her, and to my delight, instead of spurning my affection, she purred with contentment as I ran my hand over her silky fur.

Maybe it was knowing that she was different that made her search for another home to give birth to her kittens, and she found it at the back of our house. Outside there was a lean-to where we stored logs and a small shed for coal. As logs came free from the farm and coal cost money, that shed had become my playroom, and it was there that the little cat decided was a suitable place for her to make her home. I smuggled food out to her and told her she had found a safe place to stay and made a nest out of papers and sacking for her.

I begged my mother for saucers of milk. 'Don't let your father see you,' she told me time and again. 'She belongs to the farm – she's not a pet, Marianne. She has to go back there. If you keep feeding her she won't go.'

'But she's hungry,' I protested.

My mother sighed. 'Her job is to catch mice and if she's not hungry she won't do it.' But she still pretended not to notice when I smuggled scraps out.

I would place the saucer down and watch with delight as her little pink tongue lapped at the milk. I loved the dainty way she cleaned herself, even the way she stretched, and best of all I loved the feeling of her fur under my hand and the sound of her loud purring.

I christened her Snowy and it seemed in no time at all she recognized her name and came when I called it.

'She's an outside cat,' my mother said sternly, ignoring the fact that Snowy slept in the small shed.

Snowy grew plumper. 'She's having kittens,' my mother told me. She shook her head at my plea to let the little cat come into the warmth of our kitchen to give birth.

The kittens were born in the middle of the night. I found them when, as I did every morning, I waited for my father to leave for work, then slipped out of the house and made my way to the little shed. Snowy lay on her side, with the four tiny kittens, two tabby, one ginger and one, like her, pure white, suckling on her teats. Every day for the next week I watched the tiny bundles of fluff with growing delight.

'When will their eyes open?' I wondered. I never found out. I had grown careless in my haste to watch the small family. I had forgotten that on Saturdays, although my father left for work early, he returned for his breakfast. I was not in sight playing in the garden nor was I in the house and he, seeing my mother's nervousness when he inquired if I was still in bed, went in search of me.

I was crouching by the white cat stroking her, blissfully unaware of him approaching until I heard his voice and looked up into his furious face.

'What do you think you're playing at?' he shouted.

Without waiting for a response, he continued. 'Well, they're not staying.'

Tears rained down my cheeks as I pleaded for him to leave them alone.

This just enraged him more. His hand raised and came down with a thump on my back and sent me sprawling.

'Are you telling me what to do, eh? You need a lesson, you do, Marianne.'

He stomped off into the house and for a moment I thought I had won.

But when I saw him return with a sack in his hand I realized what he had in mind.

His large hand scooped the kittens up and threw them mewing pitifully into it.

'This is your fault, Marianne,' he said as he grabbed my arm and propelled me into the lane, across a field and to where a pond was.

Reaching it, his arm swung back then forward and he released the sack. It spun out across the water then fell, and as I watched it sink my ears filled with the pitiful wail of the kittens' cries; a sound that rang in my ears hours after they had drowned.

I put my hands over my ears, trying to block out the sound. My mouth opened as a desperate howl of disbelief and grief left it. Tears rained down my face, blinding me, and snot trickled from my nose as I screamed 'No'.

'You can stop that noise right now,' he said angrily to me, giving me a quick swipe across the top of my legs. I ran from him, then back to where the white cat had been. I wanted to tell her how sorry I was, how I had loved her babies, but as she saw me approach her green eyes glittered before she turned and slunk away.

She never visited me again.

My mother just looked helplessly at me when we returned, and I blamed her almost as much as him. Why had she not stood up for me just once? I asked myself.

That night as I lay in my bed with tears coursing down my cheeks, all I could see was Snowy's little face staring unblinkingly at me before she disappeared. I felt something akin to hatred for my parents then. I was never praised, never made to feel special no matter how good I was. All I had asked for was to feed the cat. I thought of that one day, the day I had felt so happy and leant over my bed to pull out the cherished dress from the paper it was wrapped in. Holding it to my face I smelt the lingering scent of happiness. But that night its magic failed to work. Instead I felt sadness, almost a foreboding of what was to come.

Still crying, I fell asleep with the thought running through my head that there had only been one person since the wedding who had said I was special.

The next morning I went in search of the man next door.

He listened patiently to my tale of woe but said very little of how he felt about my father's actions. Instead he knelt down so that his eyes were on a level with mine, rested his hand gently on my waist and told me all about the fairies that lived near the pond. They watched over tiny creatures like the frogs and baby ducks and they would not have let the kittens suffer.

He explained that they would have been carried on fairy wings to cat heaven where the streams run with milk, the mice were their friends and the sun always shone.

His words and the pictures he drew with them comforted me but I did not forgive my father and the man next door never suggested that I should.

He already had my affection; now the way was clear for him to gain control. His acquiring of power over me was a gradual thing, an insidious dominance that eventually sapped my will power, until pleasing him became of paramount importance.

Once he knew that, he also knew that I would never talk, and once confident in my submissiveness he would change towards me. But I was not to know that then.

Chapter Thirteen

When I heard the children at school talking about their weekends, their bicycles, their games and even the books they had started reading, I knew I could not share what I liked doing the most. Nor could I write an essay on it when the teacher asked us to write down what we had done in our free time.

So I never told them that, when I managed to escape from watching my brother or helping my mother with the chores, my feet would take me through the gate and down the country lane into the fields where treasures lay hidden from the casual eye, but not from me.

Once there I carefully searched the hedges hoping to see a nest of tiny speckled eggs or even another one filled with tiny fledglings. And when I found them I would be as quiet as I could so as not to scare off the mother bird from returning. I knew never to touch them, for if I did the nest would be abandoned and the chicks would starve to death.

At school I heard the boys boasting about the birds' eggs they had collected. I wanted to tell them that they were killing baby birds but I knew that if I did they would laugh at me or even worse pull my hair and call me stinky. So I never told them that either.

On warm days when nothing disturbed the drowsy peace of the countryside I would pick handfuls of tiny wild strawberries that grew under the hedgerows. I would lie on my back eating them as I sleepily watched brilliantly coloured butterflies and bees searching for pollen. Once I forgot the minutes slipping by as I watched the activity in an anthill. I marvelled at the business of the thousands of ants living in that colony and wondered how anything so minute could build, compared to their size, such a vast home. But my favourite place was the pond.

It was the man next door who, a few days after we had moved in, showed me how to make a net from a piece of muslin and a twig. He then showed me how to scoop up some of the frogspawn and gave me a bowl to put it in. He explained that I could then watch it turn into tadpoles that in turn would, after a few weeks, become frogs.

'You can keep it in my shed,' he had said, thus forming an alliance that added to the gulf between my parents and me. 'Watch the tadpoles grow until they are a decent size and then we'll release them.'

I added pond plants and small stones to the bowl and over the next three weeks watched as the tiny black dots lengthened and became recognizable shapes.

It took until after the end of the Easter holidays for the miniature eel-like things to become tadpoles, complete with wriggling tails. Wanting them to feel at home and have room to grow, I exchanged their small bowl for a larger one and placed more plants from the pond in it.

When we thought they were big enough to be safe from the fish we took them back to the pond. Over the warm days of early summer I saw them change again from black wriggly tadpoles into browny-green froglets that jumped, swam and lay basking in the sunshine on the stones or hidden by the long grass around the pool. As I watched them, I wondered which were the ones that we had helped turn into those little creatures.

At first, after the kittens had been drowned, I had not been able to bring myself to go there. I could picture them all too clearly in their watery grave, but after the man next door told me about cat heaven and said that the kittens would not want me to be sad any more I felt better about it.

And that was another thing I never told my teacher: about the times he would be waiting for me there.

When the summer holidays finally arrived and I knew there was no school for six weeks, all I could think of was the days I could spend with our neighbours.

As though reading my mind, my father quickly let me know that, whereas I might not have to go to school, I need not look upon those six weeks as holiday time.

'You are to help your mother,' he told me sternly the moment he saw me move to the door on my first morning of what up to then I had believed was freedom. 'You're in charge of your brother. You're old enough.'

When I told the man next door, he simply ruffled my hair and said we would take his two and my brother with us to the pond. 'We'll have a picnic. It will get the children out of my wife and your mother's way.'

A pushchair and his shoulders were enough to transport the three children, while I, bringing up the rear, would carry a bag filled with soft drinks, slices of cake and biscuits.

There were days when we would sit and he would put his head lightly on my shoulder and tell me he was tired.

'You must be all-in too, Marianne, having to help your mother like you do. Lie down and put your head in my lap.' And happily I did. Those early days as I listened to the sound of the summer countryside, the hum of insects, the chirping of birds, the small splashes of water and the rustle of leaves and grass, I wriggled with pleasure at the soothing movements of his hands. They stroked my back, traced each vertebra of my spine, stroked my neck, ran lightly through my hair and gently caressed my cheeks.

Nearby the three toddlers, with their faces crammed with sweets and their leading reins holding them securely and safe from the water, gurgled contentedly as I curled my body up even tighter against him, blissfully content to feel safe and cared for at last.

It was on one of those warm sunny days, when for once the two women had taken the toddlers into town, that he kissed me for the first time. I was sitting with my arms wrapped round my knees, my head down, as I peered into the murky water of the pond hoping to see something moving.

'Marianne, do you know how fairies kiss?' he asked.

I giggled, as little girls faced with an embarrassing question from an adult tend to do.

'No,' I replied.

'Close your eyes and I'll show you.'

I felt the feathery strokes of eyelashes sweeping across my cheek and when I opened my eyes I saw a flash of white teeth as he smiled at me.

He placed his arm around my shoulders and gently drew me to him as he lay back on the grass.

'Do you know how grown-ups kiss?'

I shook my head.

'Shall I show you then?' and his hand brushed my hair, then held my chin lightly.

I felt my eyes blink: as his face loomed closer and closer towards mine it got bigger and bigger. For a few seconds, as it hovered above mine, it blocked out the light and I no longer saw the face I knew so well, but that of a stranger – a stranger who frightened me.

His mouth, so much larger than mine, sucked at my lips, drawing them wetly in, while his hand tightened on my head and his fingers slid down my spine. They stroked my bottom, then rested heavily against it, holding me even firmer into place. He tipped me backwards, his weight pressing heavily against my small body. His tongue forced its way between my teeth and slid into my mouth and I felt salvia trickling down my chin. I was pinned under him, my breath left my body in small gasps and my legs tried to kick out as, panic-stricken, I struggled to be free.

And he, recognizing maybe not just my fear but the seeds of repugnance, abruptly released me, sat upright and wiped his mouth with the back of his hand.

Tears gathered in the corner of my eyes and threatened to spill over and, seeing them, he softly wiped my face.

'Didn't you like that, Marianne?' he asked. 'It means that you are very special to me. You want to be special, don't you?'

The gentleness of his hand stroking my head, his comforting warmth and the familiar tones of his voice all combined to calm me, and suddenly that was all that mattered.

'Yes,' I replied, but he and I both knew I had answered the second question not the first.

That day another little milestone was passed and the first step taken; a step that started changing his friendship into something darker. Lulled by the warmth of his hands, the sound of his voice soothing me and my desire to be cared for, I did not realize then how dark it was going to become.

Chapter Fourteen

With a family that did not encourage reading or in fact have any books in the house, I found the written word difficult to decipher. But when, in my seventh year, our teacher showed the class the illustrations in Beatrix Potter's *Peter Rabbit* before reading us extracts of his adventures, I was captivated. Those illustrations, which showed the magical world of furry, feathered and smooth creatures dressed in Victorian clothes, who inhabited a fantasy animal kingdom, cast a spell over me. For the first time I hung on to every word of a story and listened open mouthed to the escapades of Peter's family. For once the words did not just float meaninglessly in the air above my head.

When more of those books were read to the class I saw pictures of dancing frogs, talking ducks, squirrels and birds; in fact every animal that I sought out in the fields was in the pages of Beatrix Potter's books. Reading might have been difficult for me to master, but in the moments of peace that I got to myself I let my imagination run riot.

I made up my own tales of another furry family, the mice that, instead of living at the root of a very big fir tree as Peter's had done, wintered behind our skirting boards and spent their summers in the golden cornfields.

I gave them names: as opposed to Mopsy, Flopsy, Cottontail and Peter they were Millie, Maisy, Squeaker and Jim. I painted pictures of them in my head and dressed them in modern clothes. I made up stories of their lives, sending the little ones to mice school, the father to work, and had the mother always baking cakes.

I tried to share my stories with my mother, only to hear words like 'vermin' and 'traps' so I decided to confide in my dolls instead.

I would sit my two rag dolls and Belinda down, pour their pretend tea into buttercup heads and give them imaginary cakes on tiny stones. My fingers would move in time with my mouth as, using a cotton reel and strands of wool, I knitted them rope scarves.

Until I grew to know the man next door I only had them to confide in, but it was not long before he was listening to my stories too, as we sat by the pond.

He heard them with seeming interest and praised them. He told me that when I was older I should write them down and, encouraged, I looked for more to interest my admiring audience of one.

At the farm where my father worked there was a dilapidated old single-storey cottage where farm equipment was stored and birds built nests in the rafters. Once, when the farm was just a smallholding, it had housed the family that had worked the land. I first asked questions of the farmer, my father and the man next door, and then started weaving stories about how life had been many years before I was born.

I volunteered to collect the eggs, and once I arrived at the farm I would first slip into the cottage's dark interior and search there for clues to how the people had once lived.

There was a dark yellow stain streaked with grey and black, which started in the middle of the wall and rose all the way up to the rafters. I knew that was where the old log-fuelled cooking range had once stood. I liked to imagine the family cooking their meals on it and, once they had finished, opening the top to warm the room.

Each time I entered the house I wove more and more stories about them all, then placed them between the covers of the book in my imagination.

In my mind's eye there was a dark-haired woman, two sons about my age and a man who was at home every night. I visualized them sitting happily together eating their evening meal while the warm glow of an oil lamp radiated through the room.

The man next door had told me that life was hard then and that working people only had the Sabbath and Christmas Day set aside for rest.

So knowing that, I made my make-believe family work hard six days a week but on Sundays they donned their best clothes and went to church in a horse-drawn buggy.

I never noticed the time slipping away as I lost myself in my dreams of another era until I returned home and my mother scolded me for my lateness.

The man next door was the only person I shared those stories with, but I was not to know how he stored them up in his memory ready to use.

It took until after the end of the holidays for him to put that information to good use. Over the months since we had moved he had worked at perfecting his role as the perfect neighbour.

'Do you want anything fetching from the shops?' was his question every time he went into the village on an errand for Dora. My mother always responded with a smile of thanks.

'Such a kind man. His wife's a lucky woman,' she said repeatedly.

Whenever there was something she wanted he would invite me to go with him.

'Bring Stevie for the ride,' he would say. 'Give your mum a bit of a break.' And, of course, my mother never objected.

'Let's stop for a moment,' was his frequent suggestion when we reached the wooded area. His arms would go round me and tiny kisses rained down on my cheeks.

'Do you like that?' he would ask as his hand stroked my back gently, and to begin with I did.

Gradually, just a little bit at a time, the nature of his kisses changed. There were no more fairy kisses of eyelashes brushing across my cheek; instead there were more of the 'Let me show you how grown-ups kiss', and I already knew that I did not like the way grown-ups did it.

When his tongue forced its way through my lips it felt so huge, so slimy, that I was scared. 'What would happen if it slid deeper into my throat and made me choke?' was the question I asked myself as I wondered if I would be able to breathe if that happened. I felt my body tense when his hand moved to my legs. I wanted them to stroke my back but they never did any more; instead they crept under my dress and slid up my skinny bare thighs. I would feel his fingers getting closer and closer to my knickers and clasped my legs together as tightly as possible, but his determined fingers always managed to creep under the elastic before he stopped.

'Do you like that, Marianne?' he would ask each time and I was too frightened of his displeasure to tell him 'No'.

If I delayed in answering him correctly a look of disappointment would appear on his face and, wanting to please him, I would do as he asked, throw my arms round his neck and whisper 'yes', then kiss him on the cheek.

That was the second step taken.

Chapter Fifteen

Somehow hearing the words that I was hungry for, words that told me I was special, were no longer enough to halt the unease I was beginning to feel. I wished there was someone whom I could ask if it was true that what we did was right. Or maybe I wanted someone to make him stop because I knew I couldn't without making him angry and making him stop liking me. But who? I asked myself despairingly. Of course my dilemma was always whether I wanted to lose his companionship, for then I still believed he was my friend.

Instinctively I understood that this was not something to be talked about. And whom could I go to in any case? What I decided to do instead was avoid him.

Naively I believed that those words he had whispered to me for so long were genuine: that I was special to him, that he missed me when he did not see me, that I was his little lady. Believing that, I thought withholding my company from him would make him miss me. Then he would want to make me happy again and stop making me do things I did not want to.

But I was only just eight and did not understand that my wiles were useless when pitted against a man in his mid-thirties, and to my chagrin he appeared completely unperturbed by my absence. I had expected him to knock on our door and ask me how I was, or if I wanted to help polish his car, go for a walk with his dogs or just bring my brother over to play, but he did none of those things. I watched him from my bedroom window, head down, working on a car, and after what seemed like months but was probably barely a couple of weeks, my willpower broke. Out of the house I went and nervously approached him.

I cleared my throat, hoping he would look up with a smile. But for the first time ever he did not respond with his customary wide smile of greeting. He acted as though he was, if not unaware, then indifferent to my presence. I stood there for a moment feeling that I was being ignored, and then in a tiny voice asked if there was anything I could do to help.

He raised his head slowly without a flicker of a smile and looked at me dismissively.

'No, Marianne, I don't think so. You are still a little girl. I thought you were different but you aren't. I don't want help from little girls, so run along and play now.'

I felt something cold in the pit of my stomach that made me tremble.

All thought of what I had been trying to achieve left my mind. I was scared then, scared that he meant it, for if he was no longer my friend then who did I have?

'I'm not just a little girl,' I managed to reply as, with head down, I shifted from foot to foot.

'Well, if you are not a little girl who are you then?' he asked. But I had no answer for that and just hung my head.

'Well, are you my little lady then?'

'Yes,' I replied, and he smiled at the victory that had taken him such a short time to win.

That was another boundary pushed to the limit, and another step was taken.

I once heard a famous actress say in an interview that we have to experience misery to appreciate the times when we find happiness. I think that she got that sentiment wrong. We don't know how unhappy we are until we experience the opposite emotion. We only feel the need to be loved once we have experienced it and, at eight, I knew I did not want to lose affection from the first person who had shown it to me.

I had no understanding of what was really happening, that he was watering the seeds of my dependence with his kind words and caresses, nurturing my need for his friendship.

But it was when I met the man with no legs that the biggest step of my childhood was taken.

Chapter Sixteen

It only took a week for my confusion to return. We were parked in the woodland area, and once again I had done something I did not want to. This time there had been little of the gentle stroking and the cuddles that I liked. Instead his hand had gripped my head and forced it firmly against his chest and my hand had been pushed down into his lap. I did not hear the gentle voice murmuring endearments into my ear but instead the sound of deep grunts that left his mouth as his body stiffened against mine.

A warm sticky fluid spread under my fingers, then clung to them. A sour smell rose into the air. I held my breath, not wanting to breathe it in.

He lifted my wet hand up to my mouth, forcing one of my fingers into it.

'Suck, Marianne, you'll like it,' he said, watching me closely. My finger tasted salty and the odd smell had come even closer to my nose. I tried to pull it from my mouth and he laughed. For the first time since I had met him I felt his laughter was not with me but at me.

Those treacherous tears of mine had flooded my eyes, overspilled and trickled down my cheek. My face was turned from his but I could feel the warmth of his body next to me on the car seat, hear his breathing, smell his aftershave and hear his voice.

'Come on, little lady! Don't be a silly little girl. Come on, look at me.'

His fingers went under my chin, turned my face towards him and tilted it upwards until his eyes looked into mine.

'Marianne, have you seen your baby brother without his clothes?'

'Yes,' I whispered.

'Well, what do boys have down there?' And he pointed to that something that still flopped outside his trousers, that something that he wanted me to hold, that something that I had just seen grow as though it had a life of its own.

Still I couldn't speak. I wanted him to put it away. It did not look like the little winkle that my brother had.

But he didn't. Instead his voice, light and slightly amused, continued.

'One of those, you silly girl. Every little boy has one, you know. It's just that I'm a man, so it's bigger. You'll enjoy touching it soon. It's what big girls like to do.'

I knew I wouldn't. I had not liked its hard hot feel as it pressed against my stomach, nor had I liked the way it leaked all over my hand. But I could not find the words to explain how I felt.

He saw the confusion in my face and returned in a split second to being my friend, the man who cared for me.

My fingers were wiped clean, my head was stroked, my hair was smoothed back in place and a sweet found its way from his glove compartment into my mouth.

He came to our house later that evening. 'Got to go into town to see someone. Thought I would get us all a fish supper after,' he said to my mother.

He laughingly waived aside her protests that she could not let him pay for it. 'Don't worry your head about that. I had a bit of a windfall this afternoon so it's my treat. I'll get enough for everyone. You can bring the kids over to mine. We'll eat there.'

My mother, faced with an evening where there would be no samey meal of stew and no washing up, smiled a grateful acceptance of this generous offer.

'I'll get enough for your husband as well, so there will be a hot dinner for him when he returns. With nothing more for you to do, you can just relax round ours with Dora. I'll only be with this chap about half an hour or so. I'll take Marianne to help carry everything, if that's all right.'

'I don't want to go,' I blurted out.

'Whatever's got into you, Marianne?' my mother asked furiously. 'You just say you're sorry for being so rude.'

I thought, 'Why could she not guess? Why can't she see why he wants me to go too? Maybe she doesn't care?' My head was spinning round as to how to get out of going. But I knew that further protests were useless. All they would earn me was her hand across the back of my legs and being sent to bed with no supper.

I sighed with resentment and, without answering, got up from my seat.

'Maybe she's a bit under the weather,' he said, looking at me with a concerned expression. 'Come on, Marianne, a drive in the car will do you good. Won't it?' he said, turning to my mother.

'Course it will,' she answered, throwing me a look bordering on hostility and quickly turning to smile gratefully at him.

The man next door stretched out his hand, closed his fingers round mine and then led me out of the house.

My skin prickled with bumps of fear. Surely there would be some sort of punishment for me, some recrimination for my outburst. A slap, perhaps, for my rudeness and for drawing attention to his interest in me. But I still had no understanding of the type of man he really was. He was never going to act as my father would have done when thwarted. Not for him a show of explosive rage, followed by the lashing out of fists. That he would have considered crude and barbaric. Neither would he have considered it dignified to emit harsh shouts and a torrent of foul language.

No. His cruelty was subtle, and I was just about to receive a lesson in it, a lesson I did not recognize that night as having been given. His method of winning control was made up of equal quantities of manipulation and intimidation. Once he was satisfied that he had inflicted a wound that had cut deep, he then applied a dressing of praise and justification. It was only done for my own good, he would say. Once he had hurt me, once I knew he had caused the pain, it was he who would make everything better.

As we drove into the town he turned into a dark street I had never seen before and pulled up in front of a row of derelict red-bricked houses. Remnants of tattered curtains blew out of broken windows and doors hung off rotten wood frames, showing the bare skeletons of staircases and crumbling inner walls.

My heart sunk. Where has he brought me now? I wondered.

Seeing my apprehension, he put his arm lightly on my shoulder and smiled at me – that warm smile I liked and trusted, and seeing it, I felt myself relax.

'I remember all your stories, you know, Marianne,' he said. 'Especially those ones about the people who once lived in the farmer's old house.' Surprised at the turn of conversation, I gave him an inquiring look.

'Come on, out you get. I've got something to show you here.'

Pushing aside my misgivings, I obediently followed him through one of the doors and saw that he had led me into the husk of what must have been the street's corner shop.

Standing there looking around that empty place, he told me that as a boy his grandmother had lived in one of the houses and he had played in the street outside where we had parked. 'Look around you,' he said, pointing to the empty shelves. Then he started describing what the shop had once looked like. Its shelves had been full of jars of sweets, packets of tea, tinned food, fresh eggs and household items. The shopkeeper had stood for nearly twelve hours a day behind the battered counter, wrapping goods in paper parcels and selling cigarettes singly to the poor and giving credit to women who were waiting for their husband's weekly pay packet to arrive. As he spoke, I too imagined what that once fully stocked shop had looked like.

'See that nail,' he said, pointing to one near where he told me the till had been placed. 'That's where he hung the book after he wrote down everything that was owed. Lots of people had to live on tick then.'

As a paintbrush delicately paints pictures on canvases, so his words coloured in scenes of life in that street before the war broke out. I saw groups of scab-kneed raggedy boys playing hopscotch and cricket, rolling brightly coloured marbles and collecting John Player's cigarette cards. Enthralled by his story-telling, I listened to how the same boys earned pennies for running errands for someone richer and older than they. How they then came into the shop clutching their shiny coin as they chose between buying a toffee apple, a packet of pink bubble gum or a black and white gobstopper.

'I always liked those big stoppers,' he said with a grin, and I tried to imagine him as he was then, but I couldn't.

He told me what it was like when war broke out and smooth-skinned teenage boys still too young to vote left the street to fight for king and country. How women said goodbye to their sons and husbands and waited for news of them. He described the air of despair that hung over the street when a telegram boy was seen calling on a house, for its arrival normally announced the death of someone serving in the war. He told of the bombers that droned in the night and the loads that fell over the East End and Essex and how the Battle of Britain had raged in the skies overhead.

He described the street party that was thrown to celebrate the end of the war and how the street waited impatiently for its men to return.

'Yes,' he said, 'this street was once a great community, but now it's being pulled down to make way for some of those new blocks of council flats.'

He paused then and looked at his watch, and I knew his story telling had finished.

'Anyhow, you have a good look around these rooms and behind the counter. I'll pop round the corner to see that mate of mine and come back for you.' And before I could protest, he had gone.

And it was then that two things happened simultaneously which made the hairs on the back of my neck bristle.

I saw a door I hadn't noticed before on the other side of the counter slowly open, letting in a dim light that cast shadows across the floor, and I heard a slithering, sliding noise that I did not recognize. The shadows in the doorway deepened, then moved, and as I watched a shape materialized, a shape that was smaller than me.

The light was behind it and I could not at first make out what it was. Then as it emerged further into the shop I could see what appeared to be the head and shoulders of a man who would not have reached my waist – for he had no legs.

His torso, clad in an old army jacket, was resting on a thick mat, while in each hand he held an oblong brick. It was these he used to propel himself along and it was the mat moving with him that had made that foreign slithering sound.

Long grey hair fell in greasy strands to his shoulders, while his mouth was almost obscured by his thick yellow-stained moustache and unkempt beard.

Run, silently screamed a voice in my head, but fear kept me rooted to the spot as I gazed in horror at what looked like a creature from some macabre fairy tale – a creature that, by some freak accident, had been lifted from the pages of a book and thrown into a world he did not know, and only ever having existed with the reading of a story, his red-rimmed pale-grey eyes, where both anger and fear lurked, blinked at a world he knew he did not belong to.

I saw a monster! Hadn't my mother threatened me with them when I had been naughty? I did not see his deformity as being tragic, for I was too young to feel pity yet. Instead the revulsion I felt as we looked at each other turned my legs to jelly and sent goose pimples up my arms. *Run*, my inner voice urged me again, but I was momentarily paralysed with a mind-numbing fear that I had no understanding of.

His mouth opened to reveal both a glistening red tongue and the jagged edges of his few remaining black teeth, and from it came a gurgling guttural sound like nothing I had heard before. I screamed one long loud scream of terror.

At that sound his eyes gazed into mine and the muscles of his arms strained against the worn fabric of his jacket as he clenched his two bricks. For a second I thought he was going to come closer, but instead he furiously propelled his body around and returned through the door he had come from, leaving behind a smell both musty and sour tainting the air. It was then that I regained the power to move and, stumbling in my haste to escape, I threw myself sobbing out of the door and into the deserted street.

Strong arms picked me up and a voice whispered in my ear, 'Shush little lady,' and a hand gently smoothed my hair.

'The bogey man's in there,' I wailed.

'You're all right now,' said the man from next door. 'Nothing is going to happen to you now I'm here.'

My arms went around his neck, my head rested on his shoulder – he had saved me.

He started the car and drove us to the fish and chip shop. On the drive home I nursed the newspaper-covered packages, trying to warm my fingers, fingers that on that warm summer night were freezing cold.

I did not ask him why he had left me there. That question did not come to me until much later when I heard the tragic story of the man with no legs.

In the last year of the war he had turned eighteen and had received his call-up papers telling him to report for duty. Two months later he had returned home on a stretcher. A land mine had blown up; his legs were amputated in a field hospital where blood-stained doctors, working with little light and even less anaesthetic, had sawn off his legs. Not being able to face people who looked at him with pity and repugnance, he hid himself in the darkness of tumble-down houses. Nobody knew where his family was, and after the street where I had seen him was reduced to a pile of rubble by the demolition gangs no one saw him again.

I did not learn that until I entered my teens, and by then I knew who the real monster was. But for the rest of that summer when I was only eight the man next door remained my hero.

Chapter Seventeen

During the year that he had known me the man next door had laid his little traps and then waited with the patience of the accomplished hunter stalking his prey. He had won my trust, made me believe that he would keep me safe and heightened my need for his attention.

I remembered the day when he cemented his control over me.

The clocks had been turned back, reducing the afternoon daylight by an hour. The sun's rays had paled, grown weaker and lost their warmth. The ever-present clouds threatened rain, while the cold gusts of wind penetrated the thin fabric of my coat and blew swirls of dead leaves along the pavements as I walked home.

Each day as I left the school gates where no one waved a goodbye, wished me a happy weekend or even said, 'See you tomorrow,' I had looked for the man from next door, half-hoping that he would be waiting for me, but the days had passed with no sign of him.

It was a month after the start of my winter term when he finally put in an appearance. That day no sooner had

I walked through the school gates and taken my first few steps towards the bus stop than I heard the familiar sound of his car slowing down and his voice calling out to me through its wound-down window.

I stood still for a second, wondering which person had arrived – my friend who took away my loneliness and made me feel special but who I was beginning to see less and less of, or the person who drove his car into the woods and wrapped my hand around that hot and damp 'something' until I felt the stickiness on my fingers and heard his grunts in my ear. I did not want to be made to do any of those things that I did not like or understand.

'Hey, Marianne, want a lift?'

Catching sight of his warm smile I saw that it was my friend who had come to collect me. My face lit up in an answering wide grin and I rushed to his car, threw my satchel onto the back seat and jumped in beside him on the long leather front seat.

'How's my little lady?' he asked, giving my knee a gentle squeeze. He told me to open the glove compartment and help myself to sweets. Greedily I filled my mouth with the fizzing sherbet dip I found inside and relaxed to savour it.

Half-way home he stopped the car, but this time to my relief he did not drive deep into the woods.

Instead he switched off the ignition and turned to me.

'Marianne, how good's your reading?' he asked.

I was so taken aback by his query that I turned and looked at him uncomprehendingly.

'Come on, Marianne, it's not a difficult question, is it?'

he said with a tinge of impatience at my silence. 'You must know how good it is by now.'

'Not very,' I had managed to answer, my eyes downcast, 'and I can't read any joined-up words.'

He laughed at that and pulled out a newspaper from the door's pocket and pointed to a photograph of a young blonde-haired woman that was placed in a prominent position on the front page.

'Have a good look at that picture, Marianne. Do you see how pretty she is?'

'Yes,' I answered tentatively, unsure of why he was showing it to me.

'Well, pretty won't help her tomorrow when they hang her from the neck until she's dead.'

I shook my head in disbelief at what he was saying, for although I did not have a clear understanding of the meaning of the word 'hang' I did know what the word 'dead' meant. It was when someone went away and was never seen again.

'Don't believe me, do you? Well, newspapers don't lie, do they?'

'No,' I whispered, for something in the tone of his voice frightened me. I did not want to look at the paper or hear the word 'dead'. I wanted to go home, but he seemed oblivious to my growing unease.

'Well, can you read what it says about her?' he asked, trying to push the paper into my hands.

Not only was I a poor reader but I was a child who had never tried to read a newspaper. The only ones that came into our house were opened at the sports pages and, having no pretty pictures to look at, had never caught my interest. I knew something was expected of me and, wanting to please him, I stared at the print, so much smaller than the words in my school reading book, but I could not decipher even one of them. He shook the paper at me with growing frustration.

'Well, can you read this word at least?' And his finger stabbed at a word written in the large print above the photograph. 'It's a girl's name.'

'Ruth,' I said hesitantly.

'Yes, her name's Ruth Ellis. Now, what does it say about her?'

Bewildered, I shook my head. I knew this was some sort of test but I did not know what he expected from me.

'Come on,' he said impatiently, 'of course you can read some of the words. Like, what's that one say?' He aimed his finger at the middle of the article and stabbed his finger on another word. 'Surely you can read that.'

'H-u-n-g – hung,' I managed to whisper, my voice shaking with apprehension and humiliation.

'Yes, hung, Marianne. Do you know what that means?'

'No,' I answered as a sinking, sick feeling in my stomach started spreading through my body. Somehow I just knew this was a very bad word.

I just looked blankly at him. I could feel his anger and his growing impatience but didn't understand what I had done wrong. I wanted to ask what it was, but there was a lump wedged firmly in my throat that stopped me; all I could do was stare vacantly at him.

The man next door gave a snort of impatience; his hands shot out and before I could move they had wrapped themselves around my throat. His fingers dug in and tightened, not hard enough to leave a tell-tale bruise but enough to frighten me. I squirmed in his grasp and he abruptly let me go.

Then he told me what 'hung' meant. There was a rope, he said, that was going to be tied around that pretty neck and a hood put over that pretty face – it was meant to cover her eyes so that she could not see what was happening, but she knew – knew that she was standing on a trap door that would open up under her. She would be so frightened, so alone, and behind that hood she would be sobbing and screaming, but no one was going to help her. Tomorrow was going to be her last day on earth, and her departure was going to be a painful one. When that trap door opened her body would drop into a space with no floor. The rope would tighten until blood ran from her bulging eyes and mingled with her tears. Her screams would only stop when she had no breath left, then piss and shit would run down her kicking legs as she jerked and jerked on the end of that rope.

'And when they cut her down, Marianne, they'll take that hood off. And do you know what she will look like then, that pretty woman?'

I could not answer him. The image he had drawn was so vivid that answering tears were running down my cheeks and my breath was coming in sobs.

'Her face will be blue and her tongue will be bleeding and swollen from her biting it. No, she won't look pretty at all. And do you know why, Marianne? Why they are going to do something so terrible to her?'

Seeing I was incapable of forming any words, he answered the question for me.

'She's done something very bad,' he said. 'Yes, very bad,' he repeated mockingly.

Then, slowly, one syllable at a time, he told me what the bad thing was.

She had talked: talked about being with a man in a car, talked about what they had done there. And for that talking the police had come for her in the middle of the night.

My breath left me and I gasped for air. My hands, my legs and my head all started shaking together. Bile rose in my throat – I wanted to cry, to scream, to beg him to stop his terrible words, but all I could do was gasp for air, as in calm measured tones he continued remorselessly describing it all to me.

When his voice finally went quiet the picture of the woman twisting on the end of the rope was imprinted inside my head, while my ears were ringing with the desperate sounds of her shrieks and cries. I saw her dangling there – a broken doll, her body slack, her legs still, her neck twisted – and my body shook even more with rising fear.

It was then that he turned back into the gentle friend, the one who had told me I was safe with him. His arm went around my shoulders and his hand stroked my hair as he drew me towards him along the seat.

'Don't you worry, Marianne,' he said softly. 'I'd never let anyone do that to you, not to my special little lady.'

That night I took out my silky bridesmaid's dress, cradled it in my arms, held it tightly to my chest, buried my face in its soft folds dampened by my tears and tried to inhale some trace of its perfume.

As I tried to replace those terrible images in my head with the ones of that happy day when I had worn it, I thought of my aunt's house with an intense longing. I wanted to go back in time, to be placed in that bath full of warm soapy water, feel clean and wash away his words; those words that had shown me a glimpse of the adult world that to an eight-year-old were terrifying.

But the scent had faded and with it the magic – not even a trace of either was left. I was only holding an old dress, a dress that had belonged to another little girl who had once been told she was special. That was when the word 'special' meant something nice.

What I did not know that night when I tossed and turned at the thought of the pretty lady dying the next morning was that the paper he had shown me was an old one: Ruth Ellis had been dead for three months when the man next door had shown it to me.

Chapter Eighteen

From out of nowhere another picture came into my head – a smoke-filled, oak-beamed pub, red-velvet cushions on darkwood seats, swirls of cigarette smoke and a noisy group of women intent on a good night out: plump legs encased in tight thigh-high miniskirts, stiletto shoes, teased bouffant hair, wafts of Ma Griffe perfume, laughing red-lipsticked mouths, eyes sparkling with fun, brightly tipped hands waving in the air, and round after round of cocktails, with peculiar names, decorated with paper umbrellas and glacé cherries that were gulped down almost as fast as the barman could pour them. My mind had taken me out of my childhood to when I was nineteen and had been married for three months. The women, mainly older than me, had invited me to join them for a hen party. One of them was due to walk up the aisle the next day and we had been invited to celebrate her last night of being single. Not one woman there knew that what I had told them about my younger years was fabricated – that I had left home because my parents lived in the country and I needed to be nearer work. That I had three brothers and a sister, visited them often and had been happy growing up there.

Earlier that evening I had dressed with care, pulled on the white coat I had worn for my wedding, wriggled into a short grey skirt and a brightly coloured blouse, brushed my curly blonde hair into some semblance of order and finally coloured my lips a pale pink and flicked black mascara onto my lashes. Once I was ready I stood back from the mirror, seeing a girl who at four foot eleven had only grown an inch since she was thirteen. I then wedged my feet into the highest shoes I could find and tottered out of the room.

My husband had viewed my preparations with amusement, told me I looked wonderful and had driven me to the pub where we were all meeting. An hour later I was squirming with embarrassment when, after several rounds of drinks had been consumed, the women regaled the table with no-holds-barred stories of how they had lost their virginity. Eyes widened, the group gasped with pretend shock. Comments of 'Oh no, you didn't!' followed by cackles of laughter encouraged the tellers of each tale to grow more and more ribald. Each woman tried to outdo the others in the telling of the details of their own teenage debauchery.

Hands waved in the air, faces grew flushed and voices became louder and more and more high pitched. Another round was called for and fetched on increasingly wobbly legs. Raucous gales of laughter rang out as they recalled an inexperienced red-faced boy's fumbling hands and the feel of a car's leather back seat against a half-naked body. A collective sigh of sentimentality was given as with a nostalgic smile a first love was remembered. Screeches of mirth then erupted as with an embarrassed laugh admission was made to only having a vague memory of an event, as it had been a hasty coupling in a stranger's flat after vast quantities of alcohol had been consumed.

My hands grew damp as I clutched my glass of brandy and coke and hoped they were not going to ask me.

But seeing my reluctance to join in their reminiscing only encouraged them to throw questions at me. 'Come on, Marianne,' one of the group said, 'tell all!'

'Yes,' said another, 'you've been listening to us confess. What was your first time like, eh? Don't be shy now.'

As I looked at the expectant faces I thought, how could I tell them that my memories were different, that there had been no inexperienced boy's fumbling with hooks and zips as he looked down at my rosy teenage face before, after a few seconds, leaving me wondering what all the fuss had been about. Neither was my first memory of being kissed with gentleness by the man I loved. It was of being eight and petrified.

My memories were of bare legs being pushed apart, the rough fondling of a flat breast long before it was old enough to have even a tiny swelling, and of my child's heart fluttering as fast as the wings of a trapped butterfly, a heavy weight, guttural grunts, a thick wet tongue forcing its way into my small mouth, of inhaling a smell like rotting fish, seeing the smear of blood and slime on my legs and feeling both shame and pain.

As I looked at those women who were avidly waiting for my answer, I remembered that when his 'thing' that had looked so red and angry was withdrawn and had shrunk to something wrinkled and ugly, the spirit of my fragile childhood had climbed wraith-like out of my body. It rose up into the sky and disappeared from view for ever.

That was the day when my world, the one where I had filled the story book in my mind with the magic of a child's imagination, ended. Those pages full of pictures, that only I could see, of dancing frogs, playful mice, leaping rabbits and children from another era, crumbled. They turned into particles of dust and followed my childhood's soul to a place above the sky.

'It was my husband,' I answered quietly. 'He was the first man to make love to me,' and of course I spoke the truth. What I did not tell them were my memories of the first time I had been made to have sex.

When I read horrific stories about children and women being abused or raped, I often wondered which child suffers the most. The one who is attacked by a stranger, dragged down a country lane or pulled into a car before being abused? Then when found, in blood-stained clothes, too dazed and shocked to talk, being surrounded by adults who want to find the truth; the truth of what happened.

When I've read about those children I've winced with the empathy I've felt for them. I could imagine only too well small pale faces reflecting their fear, bewilderment and shame. If those children are, which is too often the case, too young to even verbalize what has happened to them, then after they have healed physically they are given dolls to play with as their means of communication; dolls that they play with in a room where an unseen video camera records every movement. In there a psychologist and a social worker watch and comfort as small fingers twist plastic limbs into lewd positions to show again and again what the nasty man did.

As the years pass and they grow into teenagers who are constantly aware of the eyes that watch them looking for any signs of long-term damage and they read the newspaper articles where vicious criminals' behaviour is blamed on a deprived childhood – how, then, are those children made to feel?

Is that worse than being betrayed by a trusted friend or relative, then forced to grow up carrying the burden of a secret too heavy for a child's small shoulders? To be a child who desperately wants to tell, to have a stop put to it, but lives every day with the fear of what will happen if they do. I've never been able to answer that question, but I do know this: a childhood can only die once.

The day that mine left me started with a promise of sunshine and warmth.

That autumn morning rays of golden light flitting across my eyelids had woken me and for a moment I blinked, then felt my face stretch into a smile of pleasure. Through my window I could see that the dismal grey clouds, which had darkened the sky for the last few weeks and kept me imprisoned in the house, were gone. In their place was a patch of pure blue sky. Suddenly I was fully awake.

Flinging the bedclothes back I climbed out of bed and tiptoed to the window, as lightly as possible so not to make the floorboards squeak. I did not want to wake my mother, who still slept.

It was Saturday morning. My father had already left for the farm and my mother, determined to give herself a few hours more rest before he returned and the other children demanded her full attention, had taken herself back to bed.

Outside the sun was rising and spreading pink streaks across the cloudless sky. Dew had turned the grass, still sprinkled with a few clumps of yellow dandelions, into a glistening green carpet and transformed the spiders' webs that hung on bushes into patches of sparkling gossamer-thin lace.

Next door's swing rocked gently in the slight breeze as though fairy hands were pushing it, and as I pressed my face between the curtains I watched an old mangy farm cat creep out from under the bushes, stretching as he did so.

In the distance I could see a light mist still covering the fields. It was going to be a hot day.

Too good a one to miss, I thought, quickly pulling on my clothes.

In the tiny box room next to mine I heard my brother rattling the bars of his cot, for having heard my movements he wanted my attention, but, ignoring him, I climbed carefully down the stairs, opened the front door and feasted my eyes on the beginning of what promised to be a sun-drenched autumn morning.

Barefooted, I stepped out into the garden, feeling the coolness of the grass against my feet, then with a child's unadulterated enjoyment I spread out my arms and spun round and around before reluctantly turning back into the house to start my household chores.

My nose wrinkled as I surveyed the room. Nappies lay soaking in a bucket, a coating of dust and grease had settled on every work surface and the previous night's supper dishes were still piled in the sink. The last was something I could manage to do and, sighing, I ran hot water into the bowl, picked up the rag that served as a dishcloth and started washing them. The pans I left; they were too heavy for me to clean.

But nothing was going to spoil my pleasure in the day, not even when my mother, blousy haired, with sleep creases in her face, came down the stairs with the baby under one arm and dragging my tottering brother with the other. She handed over my brother for me to change and feed; two duties that I performed as quickly as possible before taking him outside. She settled down with a tea and a cigarette to feed the baby herself.

It was when I was sitting on our step watching Stevie amusing himself in the garden that I heard the crunch of gravel and, squinting against the glare of the sun, saw the man from next door approaching. Scampering around his feet were the two dogs he had recently acquired: a small rough-haired white terrier and a larger, boisterous black-and-tan dog of dubious parentage. His two children, still unsteady on their feet, were toddling along behind him.

'Doggie,' said my brother, with a wide beam reaching out his arms to pat the terrier. The little dog rewarded him with a rough-tongued lick that removed the last lingering crumbs of breakfast from his rosy-cheeked face. Ignoring both the dogs and the two children, I waited silently to see what it was that the man next door wanted.

'Thought we would all go out on a picnic later,' he said. 'Shame to waste a nice day like this. Don't know when we'll get another.' I happily smiled my agreement. Picnics meant nice food and no washing up.

He called out a cheerful greeting to my mother, who was nursing her third cup of tea, and told her that his wife wanted him to take the children off her hands to give her a rest.

'Marianne can bring Stevie,' he told her, 'and you can go over to ours. Dora's not going to be doing anything, so you two can have a nice afternoon together.'

Hearing those words my mother needed no further persuasion for us to go. Not only did she have two less mouths to feed but she was free to drink tea and gossip, uninterrupted by the demands of a toddler. My baby sister, even if she was awake, would be content with a bottle or a dummy dipped in jam to suck and a blanket to lie on.

A couple of hours later, along with his children and the two dogs, he arrived carrying a basket full of food and soft drinks. We took our old black pram to put the three small children into when they grew tired and, with me pushing it, we set off down the lane.

As we reached the farm tracks that led to the pond my feet scrunched the dry russet leaves that only a few months earlier had been buds that unfurled to cover the branches of trees with their dense green foliage. That day the crackling sound they made told me that even if the insects, woken by the warmth of the day and buzzing round our heads, thought it was summer, in fact winter was just around the corner.

I pushed aside those thoughts of short days and cold nights, along with being in parked cars and derelict houses, because that day was a bonus. I was having a picnic in my favourite place with my best friend. As though reading my mind, the man next door smiled at me, that wide warm smile that made his eyes crinkle at the corners, the smile I thought was just for me, and I, feeling a surge of happiness, smiled back.

'Let's look for some rabbits' holes,' he said to the smaller children, once we arrived at the pond. Not understanding what he meant, they just looked at him vapidly. He took them a little way from the chosen picnic site and found a rabbit hole for them to look into. He explained that rabbits, those fluffy ones with white tails, lived with their families in these burrows, as well as cages, and if they were lucky they might see some, but only if they were very quiet and did not move.

While they did that, he continued, he and I would get the picnic ready. I should have guessed then that his talk was only an excuse to separate three pairs of eyes from us. His two dogs would have chased any brave rabbit back into its burrow long before it had even a chance to wriggle its ears. But the sun had lulled me into an acceptance of his words. Seeing the small children's lack of enthusiasm at being left looking at a hole in the ground, he pointed to the basket of food.

'Do you know what I have in this bag?' he asked.

Three heads shook in unison.

'Ice cream!' Three faces smiled widely.

'But only if you stay there to see if a rabbit comes out,' he said sternly, before giving them each a sweet and taking me by the elbow.

'Come, Marianne,' he said, 'let's get everything ready.' At the feel of his hand firmly grasping me, the warmth of the day seemed to evaporate.

That day, as he pushed me back onto the grass, there were no fairies' kisses, nor even a preliminary lesson in how grown-ups kiss. This time he taught me the word 'fuck' and asked if I knew what that meant.

'You know the word?' he asked. 'Well, it's time you did.'

Then his arm was on my chest, stopping me from moving. The explanation of the word 'fuck' I learnt that day was my knickers being pulled down and my dress up. It was him on top of me, his mouth over mine, silencing my protests and cries but not stopping the pain. It was tiny stones grinding into my back and coarse grass under my bottom; it was the muscles in my legs pulling; it was that thing going into me – in and out of me. I thought that day that he was going to split me in half, and wondered if when he finished there would be two pieces of Marianne lying there. Then I was looking at the blue, blue sky and hearing him telling me to wipe myself clean. I used a clump of grass – it stuck to me – and put my knickers back on.

'Did you like that?' he asked. 'It means you are no longer a little girl.'

But I had no words for him.

Seeing my face with the tears of a lost childhood sliding down it, he put his arms around me.

'It's what men do,' he whispered then. 'What they do to girls who are special to them.'

He called the children away from the rabbit hole, scooped out the promised ice cream from a white Tupperware container, placed it on melamine plates and gave it to them. It had melted but the children did not mind. His arm went round my shoulders again – it felt heavy but I did not have the courage to shrug it off.

My back was stroked, he called me his little lady and spooned the runny ice cream into my mouth. 'Eat,' he told me. My mouth opened and I swallowed, but afterwards I could not remember what it was I had eaten. Later, when we returned home, the little ones asleep in the pram and him pushing, I walked behind them and with each step I took I felt the place between my legs hurt.

'Well, did you have a nice picnic?' asked my mother, ignoring my lack of enthusiasm in telling her about the day's outing.

'Yes,' I replied, then went out of the back door to the lavatory.

I took my knickers off, dipped them in the lavatory bowl, then used them to rub and rub at that part he had hurt. Then I washed the bit of my knickers that went between my legs, rinsed out the traces of blood and that white stuff, squeezed them between my hands to get them as dry as I could, before putting put them back on.

That night as I lay in bed with my eyes shut, I saw the image of a woman with a rope around her neck swinging back and forwards. But she did not have blonde hair and a pretty face; instead her hair was mousy brown and her face was the same one that I saw each day reflected in the mirror.

Why could my mother not guess? I asked myself. With that thought anger mixed with fear ran through my body. I sat up, crossed my arms and rocked backwards and forwards, hitting my head on the wall, and as I did so my fingers involuntarily nipped and nipped at the soft underside of my upper arms. The fleeting pain of my own pinching dulled my anger – the anger that had made the landscape of my world become bleak, and the people in it hateful. And as I pinched and nipped I did not care that in the morning my arms would show tiny bruises that matched my fingertips.

Chapter Nineteen

I have often wondered how different things might have been if Dave had not come into our lives. But he did, and from the moment my mother met him the atmosphere in our house changed. My mother became distracted, showing even less interest in me than normal. Her moods and my father's unpredictable temper started flaring up for, in my mind, little reason.

Before Dave's appearance life had been fairly peaceful for several months. Extra money was coming in, and having a friend next door had seemed to make my mother more content and, even though she did little housework, tasty hot meals had become a more regular occurrence. My parents, although giving little thought to the buying of new furniture or even bedding, had purchased the largest black and white television on the market. Standing near the fireplace and usually tuned in to a sports programme, it seemed to have blunted the lure of the pub for my father.

Maybe without realizing, the man next door had timed the taking of his final step well. The effect,

however, was the same as though he had carefully orches-
trated it.

That particular interlude of peace was coming to an
end.

It was my father's simmering rage that I first became
aware of.

Since the age of three I had become accustomed to his
bursts of temper. They came with very little provocation
as though fuelled by something dark that was out of his
control. But as the weeks went by with little sign of them,
I had grown accustomed to his lack of his outbursts.

Then, without me understanding why, they returned
even worse than before and, with them, my fear of him
returned.

There was pent-up anger in the way he hunched his
shoulders, the way he walked and even the way he ate.
His expression was truculent, the tone of his voice always
vicious. More and more I tried to avoid him, and that
became easier as once again my father spent his evenings
in the pub. At night when I lay huddled up in bed, I could
hear his unsteady steps on the gravel, the slamming of a
door, his roars of rage, the sound of a blow, the creak of
the stairs and then finally the rumbling sound of his
snores.

But at that time I wanted my mother to see my own
depression, ask me what was wrong, but she, having
other things on her mind, failed to notice my need and I
was left to carry my weighty burden alone.

I tried as much as I could to avoid being alone with the
man next door. I made excuses that I had to get home

quickly to help my mother with the children, but every time I wriggled out of one situation another one came up.

I pleaded with my mother not to go shopping with Dora on Saturdays, for the man next door did not work on those afternoons. But my pleas fell on deaf ears.

'Oh, don't be so selfish,' my mother said impatiently when I protested at having to stay behind with all the children, for Dora would leave her two with me as well. 'You know it's the only day we can go and you only have Dora's children until her husband comes over to fetch them.'

I knew that, and that was what I did not like.

No matter what the weather was on those Saturdays, I tried to keep the children inside the house. I wanted their presence to protect me, but of course it never did. No sooner had the women caught the bus to town than the back door would open and he would be in the room with me.

'Got off work early,' he would say with a triumphant grin.

The children, seeing the open door, shot through it and rushed to the swing next door. Once again I knew I would hear the word 'fuck'.

'You are to stay out in the garden,' he would call out sternly to the children before locking the front door.

Down on the floor behind the sagging settee was his favourite place. 'Out of sight from the windows' was the reason he gave as I lay back on the cold hard lino. But I think that my very discomfort added to his enjoyment.

My mother had always told me that I could not hide anything from her, that one look at my face told her everything she wanted to know. So somehow I thought her increasing lack of time for me was my fault. I deduced that she already knew that I was doing something very bad.

But I still wanted my mother to acknowledge that something was wrong in my life. Did she not see my depression, how my laughter never rang out and my face seldom stretched into a smile?

I wanted her to ask me what it was I did when I walked in the fields or went down to the pond. Did she not see him following me; did she not notice the times he called me into his workshop?

'Mum …,' I would start.

'Not now, Marianne,' she would reply, and that tiny seed of courage that may have made me speak out withered and died.

Each time the man next door met me in the fields or waited for me to leave school and I was made to do something I did not want to do, my guilt increased and my continued silence was assured. If I did not feel that I was to blame as much as him, why, the man next door said, when tears had threatened to choke me and I had tried to push his hand away, had I not gone running to my mother the first time it happened? 'You know, Marianne,' he added, 'that people will blame you. Remember what happened to that pretty woman Ruth Ellis.'

Each time he said those words my gasp of fear turned into a lump in my throat the size of my small fist, which halted any words and made my body tremble; a lump that stifled my speech and made even my whimpers soundless. Then his arm would go round my shoulders; his hands would stroke my hair and soothe me whilst his voice murmured endearments and lulled me into eventual calmness. But at night, when the lights were off and I lay awake in the darkness, memories of what he had done clawed their way back into my mind, leaving me feeling frightening and alone. Later, when tiredness forced my eyes to shut, my sleep was invaded by vivid nightmares: of broken dolls, their necks bent to one side, swinging backwards and forwards from a rope; of huge mouths that threatened to smother me; and of being told by men in red robes that I was bad and must die.

Shame kept my mouth closed but I reasoned that if my mother asked me what was wrong it was because she wanted to know and I thought of a silent way of telling her. I cut pictures of women out of magazines, circled their breasts and that part below their waist with brightly coloured crayons, then placed them in places I thought she was bound to notice. In the lavatory I mixed them in with the squares of black and white newspaper, making sure that their colours of shiny paper were easy to see. I did not think about what would happen if my father or Dora, when she was visiting, saw them. I just wanted them to tell someone what was happening to me.

But nobody asked.

It was then my boundaries blurred. My mother had no time for me, the children at my school did not like me and my father's temper scared me. The man next door was the only friend I thought I had.

At that time I did not notice the real reason my mother had less time for me – that it was caused not by anything I had done, but by another person entering her life. At that time I was too wrapped up in my own blanket of black despair to notice what was happening around me.

When I first met Dave I had no idea of the havoc his presence was going to bring to our home. He was one of the managers at the farm where my father worked. In his late thirties, he was a tall, red-haired man with wide shoulders and good manners. His green eyes twinkled, his mouth turned up in a constant smile and he radiated a quiet air of authority that was appealing to women. Certainly it was to my mother, who was married to a man who paid her scant attention.

The day he came into our house I did not give him another thought; he was just another grown-up who asked me how I was doing then showed little interest in my reply. He had given my father a lift home from work and been invited in for a cup of tea. What I really noticed was that he spoke differently from anyone I knew. Without seeming to raise his voice it seemed louder and more assured than my father's. It seemed to fill the room when he thanked my mother for her hospitality, praised her homemade cake and then shook my father's hand before leaving.

'Good bloke, that,' said my father once Dave had departed. 'No airs and graces about him, not like some of those stuck-up boyos from some bloody agricultural college who think they know better than anyone else about farming.'

'Yes, he seemed very nice,' was all that my mother said then.

As the weeks past I saw more and more of Dave. Sitting quietly in a corner, my head down as I knitted small pieces of clothing for my dolls, I eavesdropped on the adults' conversation and gradually learnt a little more about him. He had recently moved into the area, he was married with two little girls who attended my school. I knew which two his children were, not that they ever spoke to me, but occasionally I saw him with a pretty dark-haired woman, waiting for them at the school gates.

He started drinking in the pub where my father went and, with the bicycle tied on the back of his car, would give him a lift home.

Then I noticed that he started putting in an appearance when he knew my father was out, but wrapped up as I was with my own problems I did not think straight away that there was anything strange about it.

I did not even take any notice of the extra care that my mother started taking over her appearance. Make-up was carefully applied, hair was washed and brushed, and she even started cleaning and tidying up our living room. Not that putting away a few pots and pans made much inroad into the mess that we lived in. But at least the worktops became clean again and there were no longer any dirty nappies left piled in a bucket by the sink.

As his visits increased, I decided that I did not like Dave. I did not like the way my mother changed around him, tossing her hair and giggling. I did not like the way he looked at her; it was as though every word she uttered was of huge importance to him, and, without understanding why, I blamed him for my father's frequent outbursts of temper.

Why did he come when my father was out and spoil my time with my mother? I asked myself when he started arriving on Saturday evenings, the night that my father always went to the dog races. Before Dave had started visiting I had enjoyed those times, for once the two younger children had gone to sleep, my mother and I would sit, side by side on the settee, in companionable silence, watching an old film on television.

Dave's presence in our lives changed that. As soon as my father had left, she would disappear upstairs to return half an hour later wearing a different dress, with her hair, which she normally tied back, hanging loose and make-up on her face. I would watch her peering out of the window, and when I saw a smile transform her face into that of a younger, less careworn woman, I would know that he had arrived.

'Time for you to go to bed, Marianne,' she would say brightly, without any explanation of why I had to go at least an hour before my usual bedtime. Seething with resentment, I would glare at his smiling face, before stumping mutinously off to my room.

I gradually became aware that it was not just me who resented Dave's presence. My father's early good opinion of him had changed into a violent dislike.

'Was that Dave round here?' my father started asking me and, not wanting to be caught out in a lie, but under-standing somehow that if I said yes it would get my mother into trouble, I just mumbled that he had not been in the house before I was asleep so I did not know. This was a reply that earned me a disbelieving look. Once I saw him inspecting the gravel outside the front of our house to see if there were any oil marks left by Dave's car.

'If I catch that bastard sneaking round here again I'm going to kill him,' I heard him shout at my mother on more than one occasion.

I hoped my father would catch Dave, not that I believed the threats, but I thought that he might make Dave disappear from our lives, and that is what I wanted.

But to my dismay, when Dave appeared on an evening when my father was at home, instead of the row that I expected, my father, with a friendly smile on his face, just offered him a cup of tea. I did not know the words 'coward' and 'bully' then.

Chapter Twenty

My mother became pregnant again.

There was no hiding it: my father knew the difference between weight gain and a belly swollen with pregnancy.

It was one evening when he noticed; he had sat down to eat his dinner when, with a saucepan in hand, she bent across to put potatoes on his plate and her dress was pushed tightly against her body by the edge of the table. That was when his eyes lifted to stare straight at her stomach.

A tide of red suffused his face; his eyes glittered with rage and he stared at her in disbelief.

'You bloody whore, it's his, isn't it?' he shouted, banging his fist down on the table. Hearing the venom in his voice, icy shivers slid down my spine.

My mother's face blanched and her lips trembled as she tried to force them to say the word 'No'.

'Don't lie to me, you bitch! Look at me.'

Tears spurted from my mother's eyes. 'Don't!' she screamed, as she tried to run to the door. 'It's yours.'

But he was too fast for her. His chair shot back with a crash, and food went flying onto the floor as he moved around the table, caught her by the hair and swung her around.

His fist rose, then in a blur it descended. The crack it made as it connected with her cheek made me flinch. My mother's hands lifted to protect her face from more blows and her knees sagged; only his grip on her hair kept her upright as he rained more blows onto her head and arms.

The two smaller children screamed with fright.

He threw her to the floor, his body stooped over her, punching and punching. She, unable to defend herself, curled up in a ball with her hands over her stomach and begged him to stop.

Something broke in me then. I had to get out of the house – get away from the brutal fight happening in front of me, away from something that children should not be forced to look at or hear about. I pulled my brother down from the table and, with the strength of desperation, for he was a plump little boy, hoisted him into the pram, then picked my sister up off her chair and placed her in with him.

Pushing open the door I wheeled the pram out and walked – not to where I could have got help at the house next door but into the lane where, ignoring the cries of the two wailing little children, I carried on putting one foot after another firmly in front of me.

There was nothing that I could do, nothing that was going to stop my parents' fight, and I wanted to put as much distance as possible between them and me, somewhere where those cries and shouts could not reach me. I thought then if only someone could lift me up and put me in a home that sparkled with cleanliness, where there was a mother that listened to me, a father that smiled and where there was no Dave or man next door, how different my life would be. Small drops of rain started spitting at me, and still I walked. The drops of moisture ran down my face and mingled with my tears.

It was then that I heard my father calling out my name and, turning, I saw him peddling his bicycle furiously a few yards behind me. He had come looking for us.

'Get you back to the house, Marianne,' he said, but this time he spoke quietly as though his anger had finally drained all his energy. 'And take those two with you,' he added unnecessarily. As he spoke I saw that, like mine, his face was streaked with the dampness of tears, and just for a moment I wanted to stretch my arm out to comfort him. Then I looked at his large farmer's hands grasping the handlebars, hands that I had seen too often raining blows on my mother, and the pity disappeared to be replaced by something akin to hatred.

I glared at him. Then, without saying anything, I turned the pram round and pushed it back to the house.

The two little children, their tear-stained faces masks of confusion and fright, stared beseechingly at me and I felt another wave of rage. How could my parents do this to them? I asked myself. Why had they had children if they cared so little for us? They only think about them-selves, I thought sadly. That rage stayed with me until I reached our house and saw the crumpled form of my mother lying on the floor.

I ran across the garden to the house next door, crying

out to Dora who, on hearing my cries, flung open the door. I clutched her arm and, through my frightened sobs, begged her to come with me. Over her shoulder I could see the white glimmer of *his* face looking at me, but for once I ignored him. It was Dora, my mother's friend, who I wanted to help.

'Whatever has your father done to her this time?' she exclaimed when she saw the battered form of my mother still lying on the floor. But I was powerless to do anything or say anything more than just stand helplessly by her side. It was Dora who helped my mother onto the settee, forced her to drink warm, sweet tea and dragged the tin bath in. She filled saucepans with water, placed them on the stove and, while we waited for them to heat it, fed and put the two distraught small children to bed.

Only once the bath was filled with warm water, my mother undressed and helped into it, did she leave. She gave me instructions of what I had to do, and with her departure I felt I had been cast into the role of an adult who could somehow help solve my parents' problems.

I wanted to run from the room and not have to look at my mother's naked body in the bath, but my love for her overcame my aversion and, gently, I took a cloth and squeezed the warm soapy water over her bruises while she just hugged her tummy and cried and cried.

It was three days before my father returned, unshaven, smelling of stale sweat and beer, but the anger that so often had appeared to consume him had gone. Instead he appeared beaten. My mother cried again when she saw him, great fat glistening tears that ran unchecked down her cheeks. Without speaking he went to her and put his hand on her shoulder. And hers rose from her lap to cover his.

Dave never visited our house again. Sometimes his car passed me in the lane, and once I saw him driving a tractor. He waved at me but I always took no notice. My mother stopped looking out of the window. And that smile, the one that had showed me briefly the young carefree woman that once she had been, did not appear again.

Chapter Twenty-one

It seemed that an alien force had taken up residence in my mother's body; a force that was not just content to make her stomach swell but, as though wanting to punish her, sent its tentacles into every other part of her body. It sucked the colour from her face, changed her curly hair into lank strands, gave her backache and made her ankles puffy. But even worse was the sickness that did not confine itself to the morning, but made her heave and retch throughout the day. Nor did it cease after thirteen weeks; it remained with her until she gave birth.

As my mother's approaching confinement drained the life force from her, it also changed my father. He seemed smaller, more tired; his shoulders, no longer hunched with anger, were now bowed with defeat.

I only heard him voice his uncertainty of the baby's parentage once. My mother was sitting on the settee, a cushion behind her back, her face white with tiredness.

'Doesn't matter how often you deny it, I still don't think that baby's mine. You've never looked like that before.'

He sighed then. 'You know, I remember that dance where we first met. You were the prettiest girl there. Now all I see is that swollen belly of yours.' What made his words painful to hear was the sadness in them.

'Maybe you should have told me. Told me just once that you thought I was pretty,' she replied.

'Aye, maybe I should have, but I married you, didn't I?' He got up then went out of the door. I knew that he was going to the pub.

That summer, while we waited for the 'alien' to leave my mother's body, must have been one of the hottest on record. The heat made my mother's face gleam with beads of moisture and her breath come in laboured gasps. It made both my brother and sister querulous and tied me to the house more and more, for now looking after the children fell to me.

When my mother reached her sixth month, she said she was too tired for her Saturday trips with Dora, so for several weeks I was able to avoid the man next door.

It was September when the baby was born. This time my mother gave birth in the local hospital. My father had taken her there when her pains started. He left her there and refused to visit.

Dora took me, and when I looked in the cot beside my mother's bed all feelings of resentment towards this unwanted baby vanished. I did not see an alien, I saw another brother, one that was so tiny, so helpless – I just wanted to hold him. 'Not until he's a little older,' was all my mother said when I asked. I had heard my mother say to Dora on more than one occasion, 'Please let the baby have brown hair.' I saw that he didn't. The fuzz covering his head was bright copper.

'So did you see the little bastard?' my father asked me when I returned.

I did not know how to reply to him. I knew that 'bastard' was a bad word to call a baby but I did not know what it meant.

He took no notice of my confusion and asked me another question. 'What colour is its hair?'

'Red,' I answered, and my father asked me no more questions.

My mother came home with the baby a few days later.

'Call the bastard what you like,' he said. 'Just don't give him a name that anyone in my family has.'

My mother named him Jack.

He was a good baby. It was as though he sensed a need to be as quiet as possible when my father was at home, and he seldom cried. On the rare occasion when he did I would hear my father mutter, 'Shut up, you little bastard,' and watch as my mother picked him up and scurried from the room. His cot was put into my bedroom and I fell asleep listening to his faint snuffling baby sounds, and I was often woken by my mother creeping in before it was light to give him his early-morning feeds.

'Don't want to disturb your father,' was what she told me, but I knew it was because my father could not bear to look at him.

I'd seen how he averted his eyes from looking at Jack when my mother fed him. I had also noticed that, unlike my brother and sister, he was bottle-fed.

I knew my father did not like this addition to the family but I did not know just how much until the day my mother had left him in the cot with just me to watch him. My father came home earlier than expected.

I heard his feet on the stairs, then a noise I did not recognize. A rattling sound came from my bedroom, followed by wails from the baby.

I flew up the stairs to find my father shaking the cot. The baby was red faced with fright and was screaming. My father was shouting, 'Shut up, shut up, or I'll make that pretty face of yours as blue as your bloody eyes.'

'Dad,' I pleaded, 'leave him alone.' My father turned, a sudden look of shame on his face.

'You're too young to understand, Marianne.'

He was right. I was.

Lifting the howling baby out of the cot I held him against my shoulder and glared at my father.

'He's just a baby,' I said.

My father looked away, then turned and left my bedroom. But somehow after that, even if he was not happy at Jack's presence, he seemed at least to accept it.

It was not until after his mother paid one of her rare calls that his attitude towards Jack changed completely and he went from being barely tolerated to being sat on my father's knee.

'He's the spitting image of you when you were little,' she said, with almost a nostalgic smile.

'What? Don't be stupid. I never had red hair.'

"No, but your grandpa did until he went bald,' she said.

Later I heard him say a word I had seldom heard from him. 'Sorry.'

My mother admitted then that she had been flattered by Dave but it had never gone beyond a flirtation and my father seemed content with that. A few months later she was pregnant again.

Chapter Twenty-two

When I look back at the six years from when I was seven until I reached the age of thirteen, so much of it is just a jumble of hurt and confusion.

The man next door had become both my friend and my tormentor. As I grew he now had little need for the pretence that I was special to him, and he showed me less and less of the tenderness that at seven had captured my heart. He stopped calling me his little lady and I became just Marianne.

It was only when he felt the need to regain any of the control that he felt was slipping out of his grasp that the gentle strokes and tender words would be resumed. But it was always after he had made me do something I had not wanted to.

There were no more fairy kisses either. It was just me, a skinny child with her dress pulled up and her knickers pushed down, who lay down wherever the man next door told her: the kitchen floor, the back seat of his car and sometimes in the fields.

My periods came, and with them breasts started to grow.

He liked to squeeze them until they hurt.

'Nice little buds you've got there,' he said with a snort of laughter and, embarrassed by my changing body, I would jerk angrily away from his hands.

Those times when I looked into the face that had once smiled so warmly at me and saw his lips twisted into a sneer, I hankered after those early days when he had made me feel safe and cared for. I thought it was me, something I had done that had made him change, and asked myself time after time what it was. There were moments when maybe he thought I was slipping away from his control and once again his voice would murmur in my ear and his hands sooth me.

Over those years my fears grew: fear both of his anger and of being alone again.

Suddenly it seemed to me that his children, who when small had blended into a group he called the 'little ones', became small people who demanded his time and his affection. It was his daughter that I noticed first had changed. The plump toddler that I had first seen in the playpen had become a pretty little girl of four with thick, dark, wavy hair and big velvety-brown eyes.

'Up, daddy,' I would hear her say as she raised her rounded little arms to him. With that beaming smile that once I had thought was just for me, he would bend down, scoop her up, place her on his shoulders and race around the garden, while she laughed and screamed with glee.

'Daddy's girl,' he called her, and I, watching them from my window, would feel a pang of hurt when I saw him with his family.

His two were placed on the swing, pushed gently back and forth and taken for rides in the car while I stayed at home looking after my own three siblings. I would see him return with presents and watch as his children tore the paper from them. The much-coveted blonde-haired Barbie doll was given to his daughter, new Dinky cars to his son. Bags of sweets made their cheeks bulge and the juice of ice-lollies stained their clothes.

Sometimes I would see Dora standing next to him and watch as his arm slid round her waist, then as though with a sixth sense he had felt my gaze, his head would turn, his eyes meet mine and his mouth twitch into a mocking smile before, with a small shrug of his shoulders, he would look away and place his hand on her bottom and caress it.

They asked me to baby-sit. 'Taking Dora out,' for her birthday, their wedding anniversary or for no reason but that he wanted to give her a treat, he would say, with his arm around her shoulders and his eyes looking into mine. 'Are you doing anything tonight, Marianne?' he would ask, knowing that it was unlikely I was. And on my answering, 'No', he would continue with, 'Then will you keep an eye on the children for us?'

'Oh, thanks, Marianne. Don't know what we would do without you!' Dora would add before I had a chance to say that I would. 'Help yourself to anything you want to eat and watch whatever you like on television.' Then she would give a time to come over that always seemed to be well before they left.

On those nights I would watch Dora fixing her make-up, spraying on perfume, pulling her tight skirt into place.

Her hairpiece, which to me looked like a small furry rodent, would be taken from its stand and carefully pinned to the top of her head. Her style was very fashionable and, knowing it, she would always ask, 'So Marianne, how do I look?'

'Very nice,' I would mumble, then watch the man who forced me to have sex with him kiss his wife on the neck before taking her by the arm and leading her out of the door to the front seat of the car.

Chapter Twenty-three

There were times when I was also included in the outings with the man next door's children, but there is only one occasion that has stayed in my memory.

It was when he took my elder brother and me with them to the seaside, leaving Dora and my mother ensconced together in his house.

It was one of those still hot days when the sun hung low in the sky and not even the slightest breeze stirred the air. A perfect day to go to the seaside, he had said.

The inside of the car was warm, the little boys fidgety, and I felt completely wretched. He had told us to bring our swimsuits, but mine was old and too small for my developing body. It clung to my tiny breasts and I did not want people to see the outline of my nipples when it got wet. Hair had started growing on my body and I was scared it would poke out of the elasticized bottom and that someone would notice. Added to those worries was the fact that I had been treated as though I was no longer of importance to the man next door.

That day it was his daughter, not me, who sat in the

front seat. I had been made to climb into the back with the two little boys.

What was it that I had done, I asked myself, to make him change towards me? I watched as his hand stroked the four-year-old's head, heard the childish treble of her voice, the low rumblings of his calling her his 'little princess' and felt a peculiar prickling feeling on the back of my neck.

Once he had made me feel special, told me to sit next to him, listened to my girlhood chatter, run his fingers gently through my hair and called me his little lady, but now it was his daughter who sat where I had sat and received all his attention.

I squirmed in sullen misery and, looking up, caught the reflection of his eyes in the driving mirror; they were looking mockingly into mine and I knew that every thought and worry of mine, that I tried to keep tucked from sight, was laid bare before him.

I looked away and for the rest of that hour-long journey rested my flushed face against the coolness of the window and feigned an intent interest in the passing scenery. I knew he was laughing silently at me. I just did not know why.

The little boys grabbed at my arm with excitement when the sea came into view and, as soon as his car drew to a halt, they were clambering out.

We all took our shoes off, walked in the sand and paddled in the clear sparkling water. For a while I forgot those nagging little worries as I felt the warmth under my feet and then the splashing of tiny waves against my legs.

There were donkeys on the beach and a sign announced that it was sixpence a ride. The man next door took a florin out of his pocket and we climbed up on their backs.

He bought us huge ice-cream cones that smeared faces and trickled through small fingers as the sun melted them.

It was then that I saw the organ grinder squeezing that portable musical instrument which, supported by a heavy leather strap, hung around his neck. He was belting out a popular tune that filled the air with jolly melodic sounds.

I felt the man's next door's hand on my elbow. 'Look,' he said, pointing at the little monkey on the musician's shoulder. Around us a small crowd gathered, drawn by both the music and the sight of the little whiskered creature that, by rattling a tin cup at the audience, was collecting coins for his owner.

The little animal was dressed in a red and yellow suit. Such happy colours for such a sad little prisoner, I thought.

Its eyes met mine and in their depths I saw a mixture of hopelessness and defeat.

People who did not see what I did pointed their fingers at him, dropped coins in the mug and laughed. I knew no one else asked why – why if he was so happy did he need the chain around his neck that bound him firmly to his master?

The man next door's fingers tightened on my elbow, his thumb gently rubbing the soft inner side of my arm.

'What's wrong, little lady?' he asked.

'Nothing,' I relied, knowing that he knew the answer even if I did not.

'You'd better ride in the front with me when we go back,' he said. 'That will make you feel better.'

The sad thing was that he was right.

The years went past with very little changing in my life.

Jack was still only a few months old when my father informed us that Dave had left the area. 'Got a new job up north somewhere,' was all he said, and that was the last time I ever heard Dave's name mentioned in our home. Jack was now fully accepted as part of our family and I heard my father proudly say 'my sons'.

My father's drinking bouts lessened, making my mother seem happier, but I remained wary of him for there were still those times when the attraction of the pub lured him back. Then I would hear again his bellows of rage and my mother's cries and whimpers that usually followed his drunken outbursts.

But when I told my mother how frightened and angry he made me with his temper and bitterness, she, to my surprise, tried to justify it.

'Oh, don't be so hard on him, Marianne,' she had said. 'His childhood was bad enough to sour anyone.'

'What?' I said disbelievingly. 'His sisters seem nice enough and my grandmother acts as though he can't do anything wrong, even though she looks down on us.'

My mother sighed at my remarks and told me that things had not always been as I thought they were. It was then that she explained to me the details my father's childhood and what his early years had been like.

'That mother of his, your kind old granny, so full of all those put-on airs and graces, was not always as she is now,' she said. 'There was a time, Marianne, when she was the talk of the town. That was when she was a mere slip of a girl and had a baby, your father, bold as you like, with not a hint of a husband in sight. Didn't even leave the town, like respectable girls did in those time when they got caught expecting. Not her – she just walked around with her belly sticking out, bold as brass.'

My eyes widened as I heard this piece of family gossip for the very first time. My mother was wont to still treat me like a little girl, not one who you could tell scandalous things to, but on this rare occasion she seemed more prepared to talk to me as a grown-up.

'What happened then, Mum?' I asked, trying hard to hide my excitement at such scandalous revelations.

'Nothing much, but to everyone's surprise her mother let the baby stay. There was talk that it was some rich man's child and that money passed hands, but to this day even your dad doesn't know the truth of it. Anyhow, once your grandmother dropped the baby, she took off, and it was his grandmother who looked after him then. It was her who always gave him a hard time. Took out on him what she saw as her disgrace. She certainly believed in that saying, "Spare the rod and spoil the child" – she beat him black and blue, often for naught reason.'

My mother paused then and I knew that the image of my father, when he was just a small child and cowering from his grandmother's wrath, was sharp in her mind as she continued. 'Anyhow he stayed with that vicious old woman until his mother finally married. But the damage was already done. He never forgave his mother for letting it happen, either. But I'll say one thing for your father: he married me when I fell for you. His mother didn't like it, but he stood by me then.'

But however much my mother wanted me to find an excuse for my father's tempers and his violence, I couldn't. Those pictures of my mother lying on the floor, her face swollen and her mouth bleeding, were not ones that I had ever been able to erase from my mind. I thought then that if he knew what it was like to be made scared and unhappy he should know better than to inflict the same feelings on another person.

Although that conversation failed to make me see my father in a more favourable light, it did confirm the one thing that I had always suspected – I had never been a wanted child.

Maybe when my mother first found out that she was pregnant and my father agreed to marry her she had been pleased, but that happiness would have been short lived once she found herself married to a man who blamed both her and then me for trapping him in a marriage that was not really of his choosing.

I understood then that once my mother realized that the pub had a stronger hold on him than she did, she in turn blamed me for her loneliness and his resentment of her.

After those revelations I tried to look at my father differently. I attempted to imagine a small, frightened little boy being blamed for his mother's bad behaviour, but all I ever saw was the middle-aged man who ruled his own home with fear.

That conversation might not have made me look at my father in a more favourable light but it did serve another purpose – it told me that what the man next door and I did was wrong. Hadn't my grandmother nearly been thrown out of the town when it was found out that she had slept with a man before she was married? And even with changing attitudes about these things nearly forty years later, if my mother was anything to go on, it was still talked about in a conspiratorial way by those who knew, and always in hushed whispers.

It was then that I tried to tell him that I did not want to do it any more.

He laughed, took my face in his hand and made me look at him.

'Now, Marianne, do you really want me to find someone else?' he asked me mockingly. 'Because you know what that would mean, don't you?'

I did; it meant being lonely.

Too many years had gone by for me to really imagine what freedom from him might mean.

'Anyway,' he continued, knowing that he had won but wanting to reinforce the message of exactly who was in control, 'I don't think you were a virgin that first time, were you? A proper one bleeds a lot if they have never done it before, but you didn't, did you?'

Not really knowing the meaning of the word 'virgin' but knowing from the tone of his voice that it was important that I had been one, I dropped my eyes away from his gaze and muttered that I had bled a little.

'No, Marianne, I think you had already been messing around with boys before me.'

Tears filled my eyes as I fervently shook my head in denial.

He told me that he believed me, wiped my tears away and then put his arm around me. Once again I felt the warm glow that feeling cared for gave me, a glow that stayed with me for the rest of that day, for he did not make me do any of those things I did not like, but simply drove me home.

The next time I tried to refuse him there was no teasing voice cajoling me into submission. Instead the smile left his eyes and the cold tone of the words he spoke to me conveyed his exasperation.

'Don't be a silly little girl,' he said.

My fists clenched as I summoned up my courage. 'I'll tell on you,' I retorted.

Anger flared in his eyes, his mouth tightened, his hands caught hold of my shoulders, this time not to stroke but to shake them as he topped my threat.

'Have you forgotten that pretty woman I showed you? Forgotten what happened to her?' he hissed. 'That was the sort of thing that got her hung. How many times do I have to tell you that you're safe with me. I'd never let anything happen to you, and now this is the way you repay me.'

The fact that it was him who had initiated those acts was not something that I was able to think about, far less express. Instead, rendered mute by a combination of despair and helplessness, I pressed myself against the car door, turned my head to the glass and leant against it. His arms went round me but that time there were no gentle words, no comforting strokes, just his harsh whispered instructions. Then there was me on his lap, my childish tears dampening his shoulder and my fists clenched by my side, as he pushed himself inside of me.

Not wanting my knickers stained or his smell on my body, he watched me try to wipe myself clean. 'Marianne,' he said 'that's what men do to girls they like, and they do it whenever they want. You wouldn't want me to stop liking you, stop being your friend, would you?'

'No,' I whispered, for I was both scared of losing his protection and of a world where yet another person saw me as worthless and unworthy of love.

On school days I would hear his car draw up and his voice calling me. There were no more sweets for me in his glove compartment; just him and me parked in the woods. His hand would push down on my head, forcing it into his lap as he made me commit another act that repelled me. At other times I would be on the long back car seat, my legs, cased in their school shoes and white socks, on either side of him as he pushed his way into me.

The summer holidays arrived again but the picnics by the pond had lost their magic. I had not collected frogspawn earlier that year so I no longer looked for my own little frogs, nor was my head full of stories of small adorable furry creatures. What warm sunny days had come to mean was me lying on my back while he, with a furtive look to ensure that there were no eyes watching, pushed up my dress, spat on his hands to moisten me, then, while the children played only a few yards away, entered me both quickly and roughly.

On days were the sun hid behind clouds he would ask my mother for my help in his workshop 'to pass him the spanners'.

'Don't you want me to help you? I could!' she would joke each time she gave her smiling consent. But she always said I was only free to go for a while as though she was issuing a threat.

Once in his workshop, where the smell of grease crawled into my nostrils and made me feel nauseous, he would pin me against the wall and enter me – 'knee tremblers', he called what we did then.

The months passed. In my sleep I saw his face, heard his voice and then woke to the memory of what he made me do. I wanted my life to change, wanted it to stop, but the feeling of powerlessness made my limbs heavy and my mind sluggish.

My schoolwork suffered; those disturbing images were not only content with haunting my dreams, but also invaded my waking hours, making me unable to concentrate on my lessons. Misery made my attention wander, and the teachers, seeing that, grew more and more infuriated with me.

'Marianne, are you listening to a word I've said?' would be one of the regular questions from a teacher who was only too aware of the answer and, dismissing my reply of 'Yes, miss,' would fire a question at me that I was inevitably unable to answer.

I would hear her snort of impatience and my class-mates' sniggers and feel a rising blush stain my cheeks. But however much I tried to focus on classes my mind would slip away to thoughts of him.

'Will he be waiting for me when the final bell rings?' I asked myself every day. The anticipation of seeing him and feeling special was always replaced by a sinking dread at the thought of his car drawing to a halt in the woods.

Homework became increasingly harder; not only had I not heard most of the lesson of that day but my noisy smaller brothers and sister demanded more and more of my attention.

But changes were about to happen. The first one was when a few months before my thirteenth birthday my mother announced that she was pregnant again. The second change was that my periods stopped.

Chapter Twenty-four

I closed my eyes, squeezed them tight much as I had done as a child when I had wanted to both hold my tears in and at the same time shut out the adult world.

I knew I had reached a time when I had to put my story in order, but still I wanted to push those images away.

It was a letter that had arrived one morning, the one that lay opened on my coffee table, which had awoken all those distant and buried memories. A long time ago I had swept them to the corner of my mind, but now one by one they had crawled to the very centre of my thoughts.

When the post had arrived I was sitting at the breakfast table, a slice of toast in one hand and a mug of freshly brewed coffee nearby. My husband had left for work, taking our two sons to school on the way, and I was enjoying the peaceful quiet they had left behind.

A rattle of the letterbox and a soft thud on the hall mat had announced its arrival.

Another bill or some unwanted junk mail, I thought, but curiosity made me go into the hall and pick it up.

It was just a plain white envelope, my name written on it in an unknown hand.

I slowly placed my finger under the sealed flap and took out two sheets of notepaper. Would I, had I known its contents, have opened it so casually? Might I impatiently have ripped it quickly open, or even cowardly left it sealed for ever? I don't know, but I do remember how without any haste I unfolded it, placed it in front of me and read the first sentence.

It was only six words; six words that leapt out of the page and literally left me reeling.

'I think you are my mother.'

Had I had a premonition or even a half wish that one day this would happen?

Maybe, but still I felt my hand begin to shake and my brightly painted kitchen started to spin as I resumed reading.

'I understand,' the letter continued, *'why you had me adopted.'*

'No, you don't,' I whispered to the pretty notepaper. 'No, you don't.'

My eyes rapidly skimmed the rest of the letter until I came to the last sentence.

'I don't want to disrupt your life but I hope you will let me visit you.' My daughter had finally found me and written.

My fingers gently stroked the sheets of paper as I tried to conjure up an image of the woman my daughter had become. And by that simple act of touching what she had touched so recently, I felt the chasm of the years apart narrow.

'Who are you now?' I asked silently. 'Who has the tiny baby I have not seen for twenty-five years grown into?'

Another question floated into my head then: How long has she known about me?

'I understand more than you do why you have written,' I whispered to the presence of my daughter that I felt lingered on the pages. 'You have questions you want answered. And I know what they will be. Did I once love you? Did I give you away gladly or with sorrow? Have I, when I made my life without you, remembered you? That's what you really want to know.

'Oh,' I continued, 'when I knew I was pregnant I wanted my body to be free of its burden, wanted it to belong to me again; wanted the intruder who had taken up residence in it to leave. But then as you grew inside me, each time I felt a movement, felt a tiny foot kick, I felt such love for you. Somehow I knew you were a girl. I even had your name ready for you.

'When the doctor cut the umbilical cord moments before I heard your first cry, that invisible bond, so strong it might have been forged from fine strands of tempered steel, tightened and tied you to me.

'The first time you were gently placed in my arms all thoughts of the effort of pushing you into the world and the pain I had felt disappeared. I just gazed in wonder at your tiny down-covered head resting against the crook of my arm.

'I saw the curve of a plump cheek and ears so delicate and pink they reminded me of miniature shells washed clean by the sea. Your eyes were shut, hidden by lids that appeared almost translucent. And the first words that came into my mind then were "my baby". Those words have always remained with me in my thoughts, even though you were lost to me. "So small you are," I thought, "but oh so perfect." My fingers traced circles on your back as they explored your body; I felt those tiny knuckles of your spine, breathed in the scent of your newness and listened to the soft sigh of your breath. And I was simply swamped with an overwhelming sense of love.

'Every day for those six weeks that you were mine I held your small form, inhaled that warm baby smell of talcum and milk mixed with the perfume of new skin and felt the beat of your heart so close to mine. And every day I asked myself a thousand times, "How can I ever let her go? She's mine."

'"You must let her go – she will have a better life than you could provide. You know it's for the best," was the stern answer from the nurses when night after night I tearfully put that question to them.

'The days sped by faster and faster. Each morning when I awoke I knew my time with you was running out. "She recognizes me," I would think, as your eyes, still unfocused, gazed back into mine and small pink fingers with minuscule nails curled around my larger ones.

'You gained weight, I saw your tummy grow rounder from the milk I gave you and your limbs dimple each time I bathed you. I wanted to spend all those days holding you. And every night as I gently rocked you to sleep I whispered in your ear of my love for you. That love that I wanted you to take with you to wherever you were going.

'On the forty-second day I handed you over.'

Was it easy?'

As I thought of the answer to that question the years rolled away. No longer was I Marianne, a happily married woman of nearly forty, but the teenager I had once been, standing in the adoption agency holding her baby.

I had dressed my daughter in her new outfit, for I wanted her to look pretty when she met her new parents. I wanted them to instantly love her as much as I did.

That day she fitted so snugly in my arms I wondered despairingly how she would feel when she was taken from them for ever. My breasts felt heavy with milk that she was never going to suckle. Who was going to feed her? What was her new mother going to be like? Those questions flew around and around my head. The woman in charge of the adoption agency moved forward determinedly to take her. She must have done this many times before and she must have known the torment that I was going through. I felt an overpowering urge then to hold my daughter tight and run away with her. I wanted to keep her close to me. Instead I held my baby out and let her be taken – for then there was nowhere to run to.

'I lost part of myself that day,' I continued to tell the spirit of my daughter. 'It was the hardest thing I've ever had to do. But my choice was made from love, never because I did not want you.'

'Did I think of you? Every day I've thought of you. Wondered where you were, who you had grown into, and prayed that you were happy and safe. And every year on your birthday I feel the same overwhelming grief I felt the day I lost you.'

People say time heals everything; I would say that time merely blurs the past. If memories were small squares of cloth then I coloured my happy ones with the bright hues of spring and sun and sewed them into a huge patchwork quilt. The other squares, some as dark as storm clouds in a thunder-filled sky, I have tucked behind them, almost out of sight. Without noticing when it happened, gradually those colours have blended together and turned my past into a more mellow background.

But even then there were still days when I couldn't fight the tiny arrows that, laced with the poison of melancholy, pierced my mind, almost crushing me with sadness and the memory of my loss. That was when the questions of where you were and how your life was could not be pushed away.

And I know there is one other question you will want the answer to; the one that your birth certificate has not given you. 'No, it's not my life,' I whispered, as I sipped my coffee that had now grown cold, 'but yours that is in danger of being devastated if you learn the truth.'

'And will you?' I asked the one question I wanted answered, 'if we meet, be able to understand the girl I was then – a girl from another era from you, one who did not have the choices that your generation has now? Or will you see me as I am now, happily married with a family and a life that you were excluded from?'

Against my will I felt the force of the past transport me back nearly three decades until I came face to face with the image of my frightened thirteen-year-old self.

Chapter Twenty-five

I was standing in my parents' living room where the once pretty walls were now stained with damp and the smell of stale food and musky sweat mingled with the sharp ammonia stench of dirty nappies piled high in a metal bucket.

My belly protruded from my slight form, my body ached and my head was full of just one emotion: fear. In front of me stood a steely-eyed social worker, a woman in her early thirties wearing a navy-blue duffel coat and a grey pleated skirt who, alerted to my condition by the school, had knocked on the door just a few minutes earlier.

A grimace of distaste that she did not bother to hide crossed her unmade-up face as her gaze took in the room.

The breakfast dishes had not yet been cleared away. Egg-smeared plates and crumpled grease-stained newspaper still lay on the table and there was a drift of breadcrumbs scattered on the floor around it.

All the kitchen work services were hidden under the remnants of many congealed spillages. Clumps of dry tea leaves clung to the sides of the tannin-stained sink, while on the draining board, next to some chipped cups left to dry, dark hairs clung to a grubby pink plastic comb.

My eldest brother and my sister were at school while the youngest child, a red-haired boy of nearly three, still dressed in the grubby pyjamas he had slept in, was sitting on the floor. Paying scant attention to our visitor, he continued playing with what passed for toys: a grubby rag, a broken doll and a rusty toy car. Clutched in one of his plump hands was a crust of bread that he was gnawing in preference to the aged teething ring lying on the floor.

My mother, her belly larger than mine with her fifth child, watched the social worker and me with eyes that the years of hardship and disappointment had sucked all life from. Childbirth and lack of care had thickened her once slender body, a body that before her hasty marriage had attracted more than its share of male admiration. Unsupported breasts hung slackly under a stained jumper, thickened veins drew blue marks on the white skin at the backs of her legs, while her swollen feet were pushed into worn carpet slippers.

As I watched the social worker's gaze take in the squalor that we lived in, with a sudden painful clarity I saw what she saw: a filthy room, a pregnant teenage girl with a slut of a mother and a drunkard for a father; just another sad, sordid case, one of many, in the files of an overworked social worker.

She could not see all the bruises on my mother's body of yet another beating. But she recognized the signs and drew her own conclusions.

She had never witnessed my mother's despair when, on the days my father had drunk and gambled the house-keeping away, there was no food to put on the table. Nor had she heard my mother's screams when, with an alcoholic's loss of self-control and rationality, my father had struck her in his drunken rage at the lack of a hot dinner waiting for him on his return.

The social worker, with her car parked outside and her job which gave her independence, could never have understood how years of poverty and repeated abuse had worn away every vestige of pride from a once-attractive woman and turned her into the greasy-haired slattern who viewed the scene unfolding in front of her with complete indifference.

There was a photograph on the mantelpiece of my parents when they were young. I suddenly wanted the social worker to look at it and see that my mother had not always been like that. Once she had been pretty, with a smile that lit up her face as she looked out at the world with the happy confidence that life might be good to her.

Instead I could sense the social worker's impatience to leave as quickly as she could. But she needed first to ask that one important question. I did not know then that how I answered would determine what arrangements she would have to make for my future. I could only feel her distaste for me.

'Who is the father?' she asked.

The truth stuck in my throat and fear turned into a hard lump that blocked not only my voice but my breath as well.

My mouth opened, then closed, then opened again, until finally I managed to say the same three words I had said to my headmistress.

'I don't know.'

With that she turned to my mother and curtly told her that she would arrange for me to go into a home for unmarried mothers.

'We then arrange for the baby's adoption,' she informed her. I felt my tears well up at that bald statement, made to my mother, not me. The baby was mine, but I already knew that I was too young to have any rights.

Two months later the social worker returned to take me to the home.

I looked at my mother, hoping for just one word of comfort, just one word that expressed some love, some understanding, but her eyes refused to meet mine. Instead she put her cigarette into the corner of her mouth and bent down and picked the red-haired boy child up.

'He needs changing,' she said unnecessarily and turned away.

I picked up the battered suitcase that contained a change of clothes and my worn-out nightdress and followed the duffel-coated woman to her car.

It was not until much later that I realized what at thirteen I had not noticed: that never had my mother asked me that one question that both my teacher and the social worker had thought so important.

'Who is the father?'

Chapter Twenty-six

I blinked hard. My memories of the past receded, along with it the filthy room and the social worker's suffocating disdain, and I was once more in my own gleaming white and chrome kitchen.

I picked up the letter again. Not only had my daughter written down her address but her telephone number too. I knew that by giving them to me she was indicating that she would be waiting for my call.

She had written that it had taken her several years to find me. She had started looking when she had a child as she had wanted her daughter to meet her biological grandmother. Being pregnant and giving birth had stirred up many thoughts of her own gestation and birth and her longing to find out who I was had grown alongside her baby.

Deep in thought, I slowly folded up the letter and replaced it in its envelope, but the words in it continued to reverberate round and round in my mind. The silence of the house, which just a few minutes ago had felt peaceful, now felt oppressive and I wanted it filled with the chatter of voices.

'What will the contents of this letter do to our marriage?' I asked myself that morning.

'My husband loves me,' I was reassured by my inner voice. But that whisperer of doubt that lives inside each of us continued, 'Yes, he loves you, he loves his family and he loves his marriage, but will he also love this?'

I flicked the switch on the kettle, topped up my coffee, picked up the comforting warm mug and, cradling it in both hands, walked into my sitting room. Sitting down on the settee, I was unable to withstand the lure of the past again – it felt so close with the arrival of that morning's letter.

The facts of life had been covered at school. It was the one lesson that had held my complete attention. But I already knew how babies were made. Once my periods started, the man next door had told me that he would take care of 'all that'.

He had said that there was only a certain time of the month that a girl could get pregnant. I had believed him then, but I also knew what two missed periods meant.

I told him.

I fervently hoped for kindness, a hug, followed by his reassurances that he would take care of me, gentle words that said everything was going to be all right. My hopes were dashed as soon as the words expressing my fears had left my mouth.

His hands gripped the steering wheel so tightly his knuckles turned white and his eyes flashed with temper.

'How do you know it's mine?' he asked spitefully.

I cried. I told him there had never been any other boys, but he just looked at me as though I was an object he hated.

'Look, Marianne, you keep shtum about this, do you hear me? Don't you be blabbing your mouth off with lies about me! Who's going to believe you anyhow?'

'My dad ...,' I began.

'Your dad, what? When he was hurling accusations at your mother, saying that brother of yours was not his, what did he do, eh? Dave was still walking around when your father thought it was his, wasn't he? And who got the beating instead? Why, your poor pregnant mother did. So work it out for yourself, Marianne: you talk, you make things even worse than they are. And who do you think will get a thumping, cos it won't be me?

'Nah, if your period doesn't come, you just say that you were messing about with the boys at school, and you don't know which one it is that got you knocked up.'

'But I haven't,' I protested through the torrents of hot tears raining down my face.

'Look, don't make it even worse for yourself. See, the law is you're not allowed to have sex with anyone over sixteen, and you have. So just you keep saying you don't know whose it is. That is, if your periods don't come back. Mind you, I don't think you'll get that many questions.'

He was right. I didn't.

Chapter Twenty-seven

Dora rarely visited our house. I never thought much about it but just assumed that she preferred the cleanliness of her own neat home. But the morning that my mother decided to ask me about my periods, she was also sitting at our kitchen table.

The pot of tea was on the table, the other children were all outside playing with an assortment of toys that she had brought round for them and Jack was on a blanket on the floor, a grubby dummy in his mouth. He was still not talking and, despite his age, my mother seemed content to keep him in nappies. He was chuckling to himself as his plump toddler hands tried to catch the sunbeams dancing on the floor.

'Marianne, come and sit with us,' Dora said, and recognizing the difference between an order and a request, I felt a sinking sick feeling in my stomach. The tone of her voice gave me a warning that this was not just going to be a normal talk.

But unable to come up with an excuse not to, I pushed the usual messy pile of nappies, plastic pants and a hairbrush off a chair, sat down and silently waited to see what it was that they both wanted to say to me.

I didn't have to wait long.

'So tell me, Marianne, where have you been putting your sanitary towels these last weeks? Why haven't you been giving them to me to burn?' asked my mother abruptly, and that sick feeling in my stomach increased. I was suddenly aware of four female eyes boring into me.

Feeling the weight of their joint gazes, I squirmed in my chair and remained silent.

'Marianne, answer your mother,' said Dora sternly.

'What business is it of yours?' a little voice inside my head yelled, but the words stayed inside me. Suddenly I realized that this visit had been arranged just for this one purpose, to question me.

'I gave them to you the last time I had a period,' I replied, aware of the glances that passed between the two women as I spoke.

I wanted to leave the table, run outside and be anywhere but in that room with the two accusers. I did not want to answer their questions. Even when I had talked to the man next door I had not put a name to the word that frightened me. Ever since then that word had been pushed to the back of my mind but now I knew it was going to be dragged out – 'pregnant'. But I couldn't be, could I? My hands felt clammy, my mouth dry and I looked down at the table.

There was a silence in the air after my answer that Dora was the first to break.

'Your mother told me that was quite a few weeks ago,'

she said, and again that little voice inside my head told me to ask why it was her and not my mother who was asking the questions. But still I said nothing.

'Tell you what, Marianne,' she said when she finally realized that she was getting no response from me, 'come over to my house a little later. I'll try and help you. Not healthy for you to miss for too long.'

I felt a surge of hope. If only she could do what she said, bring on my period. But that nagging worry which never left me would not go way.

My mother's eyes refused to meet mine, and the moment Dora left, plainly wanting to avoid any conversation on the matter, she rose and cleared away the cups. I wanted to speak, wanted her to say something to me, but she busied herself with Jack, bending down so that her hair fell across her face, obscuring her expression.

'Mum?' I said when the silence had stretched out long enough to make me even more nervous. 'I'll go over to Dora's then, shall I?'

She just nodded, but I still could not see her face, and as I went out of the door I noticed that for once she neither asked me how long I thought I would be, or to take the two eldest with me.

When I walked into Dora's living room there was nothing about her demeanour to make me feel uncomfortable. She was the same friendly person, with no trace of the sternness I had seen at my mother's table. Her smile was as wide as usual and her voice was warm when she asked me to lie on the settee so that she could have a 'little feel' of my stomach.

Feeling reassured that she just had my best wishes at heart, I lay down obediently, my head propped on one armrest, my feet on the other and my dress tucked tightly under me.

'Come on, Mar,' she cajoled, 'can't see what's wrong like this. Let's get your skirt up,' and her hands quickly pulled it up to my waist. She ran her hands over my stomach, and as she prodded me, intent on her purpose, I noticed for the first time the dark roots in her blonde hair, the wrinkles around her eyes and the smoker's lines ringing her mouth. There was a hardness in her face that I had not been aware of before, and I suddenly felt that she was a stranger, one who over the years since I had met her, I had never really known at all.

'All right, Marianne,' she said finally. 'I think I know what the problem is. I've got something that will help sort you out.' She told me to stay where I was and went into the kitchen. There was the rattle of pans, the noise of cupboards being opened and shut, then after what seemed like ages she came back carrying a tray. When I saw what was on it I started shaking. Not that I knew then what she was going to do; I just knew that I found the things on the tray repellent. There was a coil of black rubber tubing with a funnel at one end, a jug with steam rising from it and something that looked like a thick red balloon. She put it down, pulled a blanket off the back of the settee, threw it on the floor and placed the tray next to it.

'You're going to have to get down on the floor for this to work,' she said, still with no explanation of what she was going to do.

Down I got and looked nervously at her. 'Wait a tick,' she said and walked to the front door, locked it and then she drew the curtains and put on the lights.

'Knickers off this time,' she said cheerfully, as though having my nearly naked body lying on the floor was an everyday occurrence. Feeling my cheeks burning with shame and fear, I wriggled out of my knickers and futilely tried to cover myself with my skirt.

'Oh, don't be a silly prude,' she said laughingly and once again pulled it up to my waist.

'Good heavens, Mar! Didn't know you'd got so grown up down there,' she exclaimed, as she placed a cushion under my bottom and pushed my legs apart. I squirmed with both embarrassment and the beginnings of shame.

'This won't hurt. Just lie very still,' she said as she picked up the tube and to my horror inserted it into me, and before I realized what she was going to do she picked up the jug and started pouring its contents of warm soapy water into the funnel. I could feel the warm liquid running into me.

There was no smile on her face then, just a grim determination to complete the task she had started.

'We have to wash out whatever is in there,' she told me without saying what that something might be. 'It's stopping your period.'

It was then that a picture of what might be inside of me came into my mind. In my imagination I saw a very small baby, a baby whose tiny limbs started thrashing as it started to drown in the water that was being poured into my body. I remembered the baby kittens in the sack and shuddered in fear and horror.

I wanted to tell Dora to stop, but it was too late, the jug was empty. More cushions were placed under my legs and I was told to keep still for as long as possible.

'The longer that water's inside you, the better chance we have of it working,' was all she said.

Later, she helped me onto a bucket where I emptied myself.

'When you start bleeding it will be heavy,' she warned me, 'so make sure you have your sanitary towels ready. You might have cramps, so here are a couple of tablets that will help,' and she put two white pills into my hand.

I left her house and went home. My mother did not ask me any questions.

Dora was right on one point – I did get cramps, tearing painful ones that doubled me up and left me gasping for breath, but she was wrong about the bleeding.

My period refused to come.

For forty-eight hours both Dora and my mother asked me repeatedly if my period had come. I told them about the cramps and said I felt sick, but they were only interested in whether or not I had started to bleed. Each time I said 'No' they looked at each other but said very little to me.

I thought about the man next door. Did he know about the tubing and soapy water? And I wondered why nobody mentioned the word 'pregnant'.

It was Dora, not my mother, who took me by train to a London clinic.

I lay on my back, my legs held in metal stirrups while a doctor I had never seen before prodded me with a latex-covered finger. Something cold and metal was inserted into me and I started to cramp. Tears ran down my cheeks and I gulped to stop the sobs and turned my head away from them. The nurse who was gripping my arm stroked my hair but her eyes looked down at me with distaste.

He spoke to Dora, not me. I heard words 'over three months along' leave his mouth. I knew what that meant, that there was a baby inside me. I listened to Dora asking him if there was anything he could do and knew she was asking him to kill it.

'No,' he said, 'she's too far gone.'

I hoped the baby could not hear them.

'Well, that's that,' said Dora as we left the clinic. She still did not say the word 'pregnant'.

On the way home she told me that she had to go to my school to speak to my headmistress. Until she had done that, I was to stay at home.

'Why her and not my mother?' that voice inside me asked again, but I stilled it. Dora took me back to my mother, who looked at me blankly after Dora muttered something that I could not hear.

Questions of what was going to happen to me spun in my head. Surely now they will ask who the father is, I thought. The lies I had rehearsed were ready on my tongue; but they didn't enquire.

I went to my school the following day, for nobody had told me not to. I never got as far as the classroom. Instead no sooner had I walked through the gates than a hand gripped my arm and my teacher's voice told me to report to the headmistress's study where I was shown straight in.

I was to be expelled. Words like 'bad influence', 'unheard of' and 'huge disappointment' came out of her mouth in a torrent of words that I was too shocked and ashamed to decipher or comprehend fully. They filled my head, but sealed my lips, and silently I left the school without another word.

As I went through the gates part of me prayed I would find him waiting for me in his car, but he was not there.

Not knowing what to do, I went home.

On hearing that I would not be allowed to return to school my mother simply said, 'Well, what did you expect?' Before I could think of an answer her subsequent words left me reeling with shock, for she told me just what the following months were going to be like.

'It's better if no one sees you,' she insisted. 'Better if nobody knows.'

It was then that she laid down her rules. The lane, the fields and the pond were out of bounds. Not only that but I was never to go into the front garden where passing people might see me. If I needed fresh air I could go out to the back, where the lavatory was. When anyone called, unless it was Dora, I was to go to my bedroom and stay there until they left. I stared at her in horror as the thought of being imprisoned in the house for months sunk in.

I searched her face for some sign of feeling for me, some compassion, some caring, and for a second I thought I caught a glimpse of pity in her expression, then it was gone. Her face wore the same expression that I had seen on Dora's when she had tried to get rid of the baby: steely determination. Seeing it and realizing its resolve, I knew that it was pointless arguing as nothing I could say would influence her decision.

'Oh, and Marianne,' she said 'your dad wants to speak to you when he comes in from the fields, so stay in your bedroom until then.'

'Why,' I asked desperately, feeling the walls of the house closing in on me, 'do I have to stay in my room?'

All she could offer in reply to my question was that his temper might improve once he had eaten. Until he had completed his meal she did not want him to see me.

There was an hour to wait until my father returned from work, and every minute of that hour ticked away slowly. My stomach churned with fear for the one question that was running through my mind over and over again was, if my mother could turn on me like she had, what might my volatile father be capable of?

I stood by my bedroom window, the curtains clenched in my fist, as I gazed across the gravel, wondering where the man next door was. All thoughts of the way he forced me to do those things I did not like left my mind that day. Instead I remembered the way he had saved me from the man with no legs. I heard his voice telling me how nothing bad would happen to me, that he would be there to look out for me. I wanted him to come into our house and somehow make everything better. My eyes strained to see him returning from work, but when he did his head was averted.

'Does he not feel my eyes on him?' I asked myself, and again that voice inside my head whispered to me, 'Yes, he knows you are there, but he is not going to help you,' and I watched him walking into his house without even pausing for a split second to glance up in my direction. I watched and watched from behind the curtain. Surely he would come out again and look up and give me that smile, the one that once was just for me, the one that told me that I was special. But he never reappeared; instead I saw the figure of my father cycling home along the lane.

He looked up as he dismounted, and although I tried to duck out of sight I knew he had seen me.

It must have been another hour before my father called me down and, on shaky legs that seemed to have turned to jelly, I timorously made my way down the stairs.

My father was standing watching me as I descended the staircase. He turned the kitchen chair round, sat astride on it and leant his arms on the back, looking me straight in the eye. I tried to avoid his stern gaze and cast me eyes downward and studied the pattern on the lino with great intent.

'So what's this bloody mess you've gone and got yourself into?' he asked. I knew that question was just rhetoric, for without giving me a chance to answer he asked the second one, clearly also with no expectation of an answer: 'I suppose you're not going to tell me whose it is?'

That's when I knew the man next door was right; no one was going to demand that I revealed who the father was.

I shook my head miserably. But somehow I already understood that he did not want to know the name. 'They already know, they know it's him,' that voice whispered, but I refused to hear it, because the enormity of that was just too much for me to comprehend.

Dumbly, I waited to hear what else he was going to say. I did not have to wait long.

'Well, while you are at home you are to stay out of sight, do you hear me, Marianne?'

'Yes, Dad,' I whispered miserably.

'Help your mother with the young ones. But don't you let me catch you in the lane. In fact don't even put your face out of the front door. Do you understand me, Marianne?'

'Yes, Dad. Mum already told me.'

'Oh, and another thing,' and I wondered what he could say to me that could make my lot even worse.

'I don't want to see you peering out of the window again either.'

So he had seen me, I thought, and he must have known who I was looking for.

I waited for him to say something else but all he said then was, 'Now go and sit down and eat your supper.'

Trying to hide my dismay, but relieved that at least I had not been given a hiding, I crept past him, took my place silently at the table and tried to swallow some of the stew that had been placed in front of me.

The man next door had predicted their indifference. But at least I had not been beaten.

Chapter Twenty-eight

Although my mother visited her, Dora did not come into our house, and for the weeks that followed my expulsion from school and my confinement to the inside of the house I only saw my parents and the children. I could not escape the four walls, my mother's coldness, my father's indifference or the man next door's desertion. But I could seek refuge in a special place inside my head. I made up stories again, but this time they were not about furry little animals or children from another era, but about a sweet-smelling baby girl who slept in my room and wore pretty pink woollen clothes that I had knitted. I pictured her with blonde hair and blue eyes, very much like my doll Belinda. In my imagination I saw her grow into a toddler who stretched her arms out to me, called me Mum and loved me more than anyone else had ever been loved. I chose a name for her – Sonia – and smiled at the thought of her arrival. For those fourteen days when I rested my hands on my stomach and imagined my baby growing inside me, I was blissfully unaware of what my parents had planned for me.

Did my mother even realize that my calmness was because I believed the worst that could happen was over? If so, she said nothing to disillusion me.

That she left to the social worker, who came on the fifteenth day. A knock on the front door announced her arrival. Remembering my mother's instructions to go to my room should anyone call, I started for the stairs.

'Stay where you are, Marianne,' my mother said sternly and, puzzled, I paused at the foot of the stairs, waiting to see who had arrived that my mother did not mind me meeting. It did not take long for me to find out.

My mother opened the door to a neatly dressed woman in her mid-thirties whose rather plain unmade-up face was not one I had ever seen before. She introduced herself as Miss Cooper and told me that she was to be my social worker. She said that she had been given my case when the school had reported my pregnancy to the authorities. She was, she told me, in charge of making arrangements for me when, as she delicately put it, my time came.

She asked me who the father was, a question to which I just muttered my stock answer of 'I don't know'.

'Yes,' she said through pale lips pursed with what I recognized as distaste, 'your headmistress told me that.'

She doesn't like you, said that treacherous voice in my head; she just wants to do her job and get out of here, and I knew the voice spoke the truth.

Without a trace of concern in her voice she went on to tell me what arrangements had already been made for my future.

I was to go into a home for unmarried mothers once my pregnancy reached six months.

'Why?' I asked, for the town she mentioned was over twenty miles away. 'Why can't I have it here at home like Mum?'

'That's not possible, Marianne,' she said. It was then that I heard the word *'adoption'* for the first time, and as that word sunk in so did the understanding of what both my parents and social welfare had decided. My baby was to be given away; a suitable couple had been chosen as the parents. I was to only have six weeks with her. Then it would all be over and I would be able to return home.

I turned disbelievingly to my mother. Surely this could not be true? But one look at her averted face as she refused to meet my eyes told me it was.

'You are only thirteen years old, Marianne. You are still a child,' I heard the social worker say in her cool, emotion-less voice. 'You have to go back to school. You can't look after a baby and, let's be honest here, your behaviour up to date is hardly that of a responsible girl. You don't even know who the father is, do you?'

I had no answer to that, which for different reasons both she and my mother were aware of.

'You'll stay in the home for the last three months of your pregnancy,' she continued, taking no notice of my evident distress. 'Your mother wants you there for that time so that her other children don't see your pregnancy. Then you'll stay for another six weeks after the baby is born.'

Fear, the fear that almost paralyses – where breath is held, legs tremble with sudden weakness and the stomach churns acid – filled me. It stifled my voice, stopping me from opening my mouth to argue. Instead I felt limp, with waves of despair engulfing me. Not only had my parents arranged behind my back to have my baby adopted, but also they were sending me away. Apart from that night so long ago when I had been a bridesmaid, I had never spent a night apart from my family. The thought of spending so long away from them all petrified me.

The date was set and it was agreed that the social worker would return in two months' time to take me to the unmarried mothers' home. Having completed her job, she closed her file, rose and left with it under her arm.

'No!' I wailed when the door closed behind her.

'It's for the best,' my mother said wearily.

'Whose best?'

'The baby's, Marianne,' she replied. With her mouth set firmly, my mother turned away and I knew the conversation was over.

There was nothing left for me to do except go to my bedroom and try and stay as far away from my mother as I could, at least until I felt able to face her again. She perhaps understood that and did not call me down to help her with the chores as she usually did.

Once upstairs I sat on the edge of my unmade bed, staring at the walls, my hands clasping my face tightly. My fingers left little white marks where I pressed them hard into my cheeks. I felt the tears sliding down the back of my throat until they solidified into a small hard ball that threatened to choke me. As I thought about the conversation with the social worker and my mother, I rocked my body back and forwards in utter despair.

'What have I done? What have I done?' kept repeating itself in my head followed by that tiny inner voice whispering, 'What could you do?' Those two questions chased themselves round and round in my brain, one that still felt numb with shock and emotion.

And that other question joined them again: Why had my parents not asked who the father was?

Chapter Twenty-nine

The morning I was due to go to the home I came out of a deep sleep suddenly. The haziness of the light that was seeping through my curtains told me that it was too early to be awake, but something had woken me, some noise that did not belong in my room. My heart started pounding as my ears strained to hear what it was. I climbed from my bed and went to my window, where the sound seemed the strongest, and peering closer I saw a moth trapped between the curtains and the glass. It was the sound of the beating of its wings that had woken me, as it desperately struggled to be free.

I opened my window to let it escape and watched as the pale wings fluttered and the moth flew off to enjoy its freedom. I wished I too could have followed it.

Eight weeks had passed since the social worker's visit; this was the day I was leaving my home, and I still had to pack. I looked desolately through my small selection of clothes. I was not a girl with many clothes, but my expanding stomach meant I had even fewer options. Exasperated, I threw them in a heap onto the bed. I was finding even the smallest decision difficult to make.

Looking in the mirror I saw a different girl reflected in its mottled surface than the one who had been there when the social worker had called. The weeks that had slipped slowly by had changed me into someone I hardly recognized as myself. My belly, protruding from my slight form, could no longer be hidden. It would have been clear to anyone who saw me that I was pregnant. My tiny breasts, which had become tender to the touch, were larger, and there was a new fragility to my face. The roundness of youth had disappeared, leaving me with sharp cheekbones and a pointed chin.

This girl who stared back at me with dull eyes, red rimmed from constant weeping, was pale, with hair that had turned dry and brittle, and a mouth that looked as though it had long ago forgotten how to smile.

I felt heavy, my back ached, but worse than that was the overwhelming sadness that constantly consumed me. It dogged every moment of my waking hours and slipped into my dreams, making me wake to a pillow damp with my tears, as the impending loss of the baby that I already loved drew closer. As I thought of the day ahead I felt her move within that space inside me; that space that she had made hers – just under my heart.

I pictured her curled up inside me, for I knew that at six months she was already perfectly formed – that all she had to do was grow a little before she came into the world.

Every night before I went to sleep and each morning when I woke I talked softly to her, for I knew instinctively that my baby was a 'her'. I told her how much I loved her, how I was looking forward to meeting her, but I could not bring myself to say or acknowledge the word 'adoption'.

That morning I placed my hand on my belly, feeling its roundness.

'Can you feel that, Sonia?' I asked. 'Can you feel my hand touching you?'

The realness of her tiny movements and the fullness of my teenage breasts that were preparing for her arrival heightened my grief at the emptiness that her leaving me would bring to my life.

'How could they do this to me? To her?' I asked desperately. I thought of the faceless couple that were also waiting for her birth and wondered what they were like.

I pictured them in a large house, one that without the sound of children's laughter was lonely. There would be a bedroom freshly decorated in pastel colours all ready and waiting to receive my baby, a room full of soft fluffy toys with a white-painted cot, a tinkling mobile in the centre above it and by the window a rocking chair where my baby would be held by her new mother as she was fed from a bottle. Against the wall would be a chest of drawers full of lacy baby clothes, and on the floor would be a rug made out of wool, not the handmade rag ones that were in my home but a soft woollen one with a delicate pattern of roses on it. Their house would have an indoor bathroom and a patio and a new three-piece suite with matching brightly coloured cushions. I thought they must want a baby very much – that from the moment she went home with them she would be loved. Then I cried deep sobs of loss for she would never get to know me or me her.

Chapter Thirty

'Time to go, Marianne,' the social worker said as she glanced at my small suitcase. 'Is that all you've got?'

'Yes.'

She picked it up. 'Can't have you carrying heavy weights now, can we?' she said with a humourless smile as she led the way out of the front door.

I looked at my mother and saw the dark shadows that tiredness had brushed under her eyes. I saw her belly, larger than mine, straining against the worn fabric of her only maternity dress.

By the time I return home there will be another baby here, I thought sadly, but it won't be mine.

My mother stood to the side of the door as I made to go through it. I wanted her to say something kind, some words that I could tuck away in my memory until at night, when I was alone, I could listen to them in my mind and be comforted.

'Hug me,' I wanted to ask. 'Tell me I'll be missed, or simply say you love me,' but the words stayed in my head and my mother did none of those things. She just told me to take care, to look after myself, and then she stood in the shadows of the doorway watching me leave.

I glanced at the other house across the way but it was closed up. The man next door and his family were nowhere in sight.

The social worker put my case in the boot and told me to make myself comfortable. She drove out of the lane along windy roads lined with trees. There was little traffic, just the odd tractor and a few cars, but I noticed that she drove carefully, her eyes darting up to the mirror, her hands clutched firmly on the steering wheel.

I leant my head against the cool glass of the window and watched as we passed fields that were bare of crops, for they had been harvested some weeks ago. The sight of the farmhouse where my father worked brought the image of the man next door into my mind. I knew that he was out there somewhere servicing the farmer's tractors or mending the cars, and I wondered where.

I asked myself, 'Does he ever think of me? Think about what is going to happen to me, wonder if I'm all right? He must know about the baby but does he know it's to be given away like an unwanted puppy?'

'Of course he knows,' screamed that voice in my head, and hearing it a slow burning anger at his betrayal coursed through my veins, making my face hot and my hands clammy.

A couple of miles further on we passed the woodlands where the man next door had so often taken me, and, remembering that, I shivered. It was only midday but already it seemed the day was growing dark. The weak winter sun disappeared behind the branches of overhanging trees and I peered through the lattice they formed at a sky dark with clouds that promised rain.

It was not until estates of new identical houses, which told me we were on the edge of the town, appeared that the social worker finally spoke. Up to then she had seemed lost in her own thoughts, or maybe she was just concentrating on her driving and not getting lost. She told me that at the home I would resume my school studies. A teacher would come in and give me work to do, and when I was ready to leave arrangements had been made for me to start at a new school in the spring term.

'Nobody there will know anything about you,' she said then. 'You will be able to have a new start and put all this behind you.'

Her words fell on disinterested ears. How could she suggest that I could put my baby behind me?

The new estates with their square gardens gradually gave way to large Victorian terraced houses as we drove further into town. We passed those and turned into a tree-lined road of even larger detached grey-brick houses. Before the two world wars they had been built for the rich and privileged Victorians and Edwardians. These were households where butlers, scullery maids, cooks and the rest of the assortment of staff that houses such as those demanded worked from dawn to dusk and slept in the attic rooms. Now, when servants were no longer content to work for little more than their board and keep and death duties had decimated inherited wealth, the majority of these homes had been divided up into a maze of small flats.

Helpless

The car drew up outside one of these houses. Double wooden doors and a single bell proclaimed that, unlike its neighbours, it still had retained its single-residence status.

'Here we are,' said the social worker in bright tones, as though this was an outing and our arrival an unexpected treat.

I peered out and saw a huge grey-stone building with ornate carvings over the dark double front doors and each of the downstairs windows. They were heavily curtained, hiding any signs of life inside. Clumps of shrubs, turned winter brown, dotted the lawn that ran from its walls to the pavement, and I, used to a front garden full of battered toys and tangled weeds, thought it looked curiously empty. In the distance there was a large fruit orchard, the leaves missing from the trees, and I imagined that in summer it shaded the prams of the infants that were born at the home.

While I looked about me trying to take in my surroundings my suitcase was lifted out of the car and I was instructed to follow. The bell was firmly pushed and you could hear its loud sound resonate inside the imposing house. In what seemed like seconds, the front door was opened.

I walked into a huge hall with the highest ceiling I had ever seen. It had polished dark-wood floors, and on the papered walls large paintings of old country scenes and portraits of austere Victorians looked down on us.

'I've brought Marianne,' said the social worker to the woman who, with her grey uniform and hair, was almost an exact match to the outside brickwork. In my dream-like state it made me think that if she leant against the exterior of the house all I would see would be her round face with its double chin.

The woman, who later told me she was the matron, nodded at the social worker and told her that she would take over.

With a hurried goodbye my escort who, disinterested as she appeared to be in me, was my last link to my family left me standing in the hall with my battered suitcase at my side. A knot of apprehension tightened in my stomach as I faced the woman whose charge I was going to be in for the next few months.

Chapter Thirty-one

All these years later, many of my memories of that place and the girls I met there are absent. Only the matron's and one other face remain clear in my mind, but it is not the staff who worked in the home or the other girls' stories that come to me when I think of that time. It is how I was then at thirteen, with the love I felt for the baby growing inside me, the fear of the pain of the birth and the grief I felt at the impending adoption that are dominant in my mind.

I have vague impressions of the three girls I met the first day, but their names have long ago slipped away into the mists of time. The first one, the one whose face I remember, was tall and, apart from her tell-tale bulge, thin. She was aged around twenty, which then looked quite old to me. When I think back it is only her words she spoke at our first meeting that I can remember.

'Jesus, you're a bit young, aren't you? So who knocked you up?'

And I can still remember her disbelieving sniff when I told her my stock answer of 'I don't know'.

'Course you don't, luv,' she sneered. 'Bet it was some fat old uncle who told you to be quiet. Wonder what he threatened you with. Told you not to tell? Said everyone would be mad at you, did he?'

As I looked with something approaching amazement at her, I saw the malice that glinted in the depths of her brown eyes, made big by thick, dark mascara and eyeliner, and I knew that she saw me as someone on whom to vent her frustration with the world. But worse than that, I thought, she saw me.

'Or did you like him too much to tell?' she continued. 'Bet it wasn't rape.'

She laughed then when she saw me wince as her barb hit home.

After all, what answer could I give? I didn't think that what the man next door and I had done was rape, but I was not even sure what rape was, so I said nothing.

Another cruel peal of laughter left her mouth as she took my silence for an admission of something. I was not clear what that something was but knew that her mocking laughter judged and defiled me.

Other girls, seeing my shame and distress, told her to be quiet. I remember that, but I can't remember what they said, only that they were kind.

It is the home's routine that I can still recall. Every morning we had to get up at seven thirty, make our beds before having breakfast in the dining room and then take it in turns to do the washing up.

I was excused the work of preparing lunch and washing floors that the other girls did, for I was the only girl of school age and had lessons to attend. Five days a week I sat in the common room trying to complete the exercises that the visiting teacher left for me several times a week. In the hours after I had done my evening chores I sat in my room, the exercise book on my desk, and tried to concentrate on the work the teacher left for me.

I suspect that the other girls thought I got off lightly but they did not know that I would rather have been working with them than sitting in isolation, poring over school books that held little interest for me.

At the weekends I was given the task of brushing and sweeping the staircases and cleaning the bathrooms and toilets – the two most unpopular chores – but I suppose they thought that as I got off so lightly in the week I could make up for it then.

The common parts were everyone's responsibility, and should we leave behind any item, however small, the guilty person was fined one penny. As I had no money with me I learnt quickly to be very tidy. The girls did their own laundry and ironing, which was something I enjoyed, for I liked having clean clothes to wear every day.

It was while I was in the home, with its polished floors, clean bathrooms and immaculate kitchen, that I realized just how much I disliked upswept lino, grimy surfaces and creased, crumbled clothes and shuddered when I thought of how my mother kept the house.

The older girls taught me to cook simple meals and in the evenings showed me how they unravelled old jumpers bought from charity shops so that the wool could then be knitted into baby clothes. Not having the money to purchase anything, I contended myself with helping the girls roll the wool into large balls and watched how they were turned into small infants' garments.

In addition to the common room there was a formal lounge furnished with high-backed velvet-covered chairs, a floral covered settee and several small tables. This was only used once a fortnight when birth classes were given by a visiting maternity nurse on how to breathe during our labour and how to care for a newborn.

As we practised, my mind would wander. I used to think of the couples that, like us, were waiting for their babies to be born. How different their experiences would be to ours, for they would get to keep their babies. They would have each other, and then their baby would join them. They would be a family, and love would surround them.

The nursery was where the new mothers stayed after giving birth and was under the supervision of the matron. It was on the same floor as our bedrooms but closed off by two sets of doors. There the new mothers cared for the newborns under the careful eye of the woman who had also delivered them.

Within a few days of being in the home I began to fear both the pain of the birth and being dependent on the matron for easing it. There was something so cold and unforgiving in the glances she gave us that I knew she thought we were girls who had sinned and it was clear she had little if any sympathy for us.

I often heard sobs in that home. Sometimes they were suddenly stifled as though a face was turned and pressed into a pillow. Other times, like on the day the new mother had to hand over her baby for adoption, they were wrenching, tearing cries of loss and despair. I saw those sad young girls leave the home pale faced, their breasts still leaking the milk that would never be suckled, clutching their suitcases as they walked with hunched shoulders and faltering steps out of the doors and turned in the direction that took them to the bus stop. I wonder where they went, those girls who had not been collected by their unforgiving families or written to by the man they had thought loved them. I pictured the lonely bed-sitters and squalid boarding houses that were the fate of young girls ostracized by their families.

All these years later those girls at the home are just a blurred memory of large bellies. Some were angry, others sad and most were just defeated. They all had sad stories to tell; of boyfriends who had left them, families who had rejected them, even one or two whom a man they had trusted had forced unwillingly into having sex. But like their faces, those tales, of which I heard so many, have mainly become indistinguishable from each other.

There were a few, a very few times that did end with happy faces. Those were the girls who left carrying their tiny swaddled bundle, collected by a family who had relented and decided to welcome them both back into the home. There was even the odd rare occasion when it was a young man who turned up to meet his ready-made family. He had written her a letter full of remorse, and said he wanted to marry her.

That girl left the home with the widest smile of all.

Chapter Thirty-two

I was the youngest girl in the home and the only one still at school. The day I arrived I was shown my room, and because I had to study I had been given a single one. There was a single bed, a locker for my few belongings, a desk with a wooden chair for me to work at in the evenings when the common room was full. When I saw it, my heart sank, as it dawned on me that this bare room, with none of my personal possessions and memories of childhood, was to be my home for several months. I felt waves of loneliness, for already I was missing my family and even my bedroom in which I had recently spent so much time confined.

The first night I was there I was woken several times by the noise of the town: the rumbling of commuter trains, cars driving constantly up and down the street, and laughter and shrieks from weekend revellers as they walked back to the flats and bed-sitters in the road. No sooner had I become used to these sounds than the overworked central-heating boiler shook and moaned in the darkness of the night. I had never been in an old house of this size before and it seemed to groan and sigh all of its own accord as it too settled down to sleep.

Tucked away at the top of two flights of stairs, the attic rooms that had once housed the servants had been turned into a little chapel. Every Sunday all the girls except those who had recently given birth were herded up to listen to the service given by a local minister.

There was something about the space, maybe the simplicity of its plain cream-coloured walls and the austere wooden seats, which comforted me. But the words of the minister, who made much of our sins and how we must ask for forgiveness, always failed to.

The matron always followed his sermon by giving us a short talk that from week to week hardly varied. The theme was repetitive. We were sinners and she hoped we had had time to reflect on our sins and that when we went back into the outside world we would find it in ourselves to lead a better and more virtuous life.

I let her words and the monotonous tones of the minister float in the air above my head. Instead of listening and thinking of repentance, I concentrated on the beauty of the stained-glass window which, to give the chapel a more religious feel, had been set into the wall when the attic was converted.

Through it I could see a patch of sky, sometimes dark and at other times blue, and it was to there that I directed my silent prayers.

'I know I've been bad,' I would say, 'but please believe me, I'm so sorry – sorry that I have sinned.'

I would ask for forgiveness and help, not for me, but for my baby. 'Please,' I would pray, 'keep her safe.'

Before I knew it, Christmas week had arrived and even the saddest girls seemed infected by the festive spirit. We were told that on Christmas Day not only were we going to have a proper Christmas dinner with all the trimmings, but that we could use the formal lounge and even the babies who were barred from the common room were going to be allowed in with their mothers.

On Christmas Eve two huge fir trees, donated by one of the local businesses, were brought in, one for the hall and one for the lounge. Large boxes of decorations were handed to us and we were told, for once with a smile, that we could spend the morning decorating them. A radio played Christmas carols and we sang along to them. The girls, all in varying degrees of pregnancy, surrounded the trees and amidst peals of laughter the less unwieldy ones climbed on chairs held firmly by another to string ropes of coloured lights and streamers around every branch. Being the smallest, I was told to decorate the lower branches and was in the middle of hanging glittering silver and crimson balls on them when the matron appeared to tell me I had a visitor.

'The man next door has come,' was the first thought that came into my mind, but when I followed the matron into the hall to my amazement I saw my aunt, the one I had been bridesmaid to years before, standing there.

'Hallo, Marianne,' she said, and I felt tears come into my eyes.

I wanted to throw myself into her arms, I was so pleased to see someone from my family, but shyness at my condition stopped me.

We were given one of the small offices to sit in and I waited for my aunt to tell me, not just why she was there, but also how she knew where I was.

'It was your dad who told me,' she said, answering my unspoken question. 'Marianne, I don't know what's happened to you and I know he was angry, but he did ask me to come.'

I thought wryly that, with my belly sticking out as far as it was possible, it was pretty clear what had happened to me. But I was so taken aback at what she had said, that it was my father who had asked her to come, that speech failed me. I had thought he was the least likely person to have any sympathy for my plight, yet it was he who had talked to his sister.

'I doubt if it was all your fault,' my aunt said, and I saw her looking at my stomach. 'My brother doesn't really think it either, whatever he may have said to you. Before you ask, no, he's not told anyone else, only me. Your mum doesn't even know I'm here.'

She took a parcel wrapped in gold paper out of her bag and put it on the table in front of me.

'Now don't open it before the morning,' she said. 'We didn't want to think of you not having a present to open tomorrow.'

She gave me a kiss, just a small one on my cheek, and then left in a cloud of perfume. The warmth of her visit stayed with me that night and all of the next day. All I could think was that my family had not forgotten me.

If I had been amazed to see my aunt standing in the hall, my next visitor was an even bigger shock.

When the matron told me for the second time that day that there was a person to see me, my heart lurched.

Again I wondered if it was the man next door; it wasn't, it was Dora.

Clutching a parcel and wearing, for her, a nervous smile, she gave me a brief hug.

She looked different, less confident. Just in the few months since I had seen her she had visibly aged. There were new lines around her eyes and a grey pallor to her cheeks that her liberally applied make-up failed to conceal.

'You look well, Mar,' she said, using her affectionate abbreviation of my name. But I no longer saw the woman who had acted as my surrogate aunt for six years. Since I had been in the home, my memories of what I had thought was friendship and those random acts of kindness of hers had drifted behind a much clearer picture – that of her pushing a hose up inside me when she had tried to flush my baby out.

I wanted to ask her what she wanted and why she had come, but instead I led her into the office that I had been allowed to use for the second time that day. I waited for her to tell me why she had come. My composure, if I can call it that, seemed to unnerve her. Her eyes refused to meet mine and her fingers, unused to not being able to hold a cigarette, fidgeted with her wedding ring. She passed me a parcel, which was wrapped in much plainer paper than my aunt's present, and was large and bulky. Again I was given instructions not to open it until the next day. It was not clear who it was from and I did not ask.

'Your mother has had the baby, another boy,' she told me.

I gulped at the thought of my mother sitting in our house by the fire with a newborn in her arms, while here I was, all alone in this home, waiting to give birth to my own baby and with the threat of adoption hanging over me.

'That's why she didn't come with me,' she continued, 'but she said for me to tell you that when the baby comes, she will be here. Your dad's going to borrow a car so he can drive her here. She will leave the new baby with me.'

'And the man next door?' I thought, noticing that not once was his name mentioned, not even with a 'we' or an 'us'.

I guessed it was he who was lending Dad the car, but said nothing. It was clear that the man next door had disappeared from my life as much as he could, and again I felt cold pangs of hurt at his betrayal.

'Does he know that his wife has come?' I wondered, and that voice inside my head, the one that constantly reminded me of the truth, whispered, 'Of course he does. He knows everything, and so does she.'

Dora carried on trying to make conversation, an effort that rapidly turned her attempts into a nervous monologue, for I could not bring myself to respond. I had numerous questions I wanted to ask formulating in my head. What is the new baby like? How are my brothers and my sister? Do they ask my mother where I am? Am I missed? And the last one that had become fixed in my mind ever since it was she and not my mother who had asked where I had put my sanitary towels: How long have you known? Not being able to summon up the courage to ask the last question, I swallowed all the others.

She, sensing that I was lost to her, finished speaking and, with a look of relief that her duty was done, rose to leave.

'Be nice to have you back home,' she said, but I knew she was not speaking the truth. 'Won't be long now,' and for the first time her eyes slid to my stomach.

She gathered up her belongings – a woollen scarf thrown carelessly over the back of the chair, a pair of worn leather gloves, and finally her handbag. She gave me a quick kiss on my cheek with lips that felt dry and cold, then left. I stood at the door watching her retreating back until she had disappeared from view, then I shut the front door softly.

I went back to the lounge, picked up a silver ball and placed it carefully on the tree.

Chapter Thirty-three

*L*ater on Christmas Eve, after we had had supper and done the washing up, we all went to the chapel where the minister talked about forgiveness and the birth of Jesus, but to everyone's relief the matron for once refrained from making her usual speech. Through the twinkling window I could see the moon and the stars and I laid my hand on my stomach and thought about my baby.

That night I found it difficult to go to sleep. All I could think about was my family and how much I missed them. I wondered what they would do on Christmas Day and if they would miss me. The fact that they had not forgotten me brought a smile of pleasure to my face. But when I thought of my brothers and sister I just wanted to be with them. I pictured my mother holding the new baby and remembered how my father had smiled with pride when my oldest brother was born. Was he the same with this one? I wondered. I thought he most probably was.

When I did finally fall asleep the noise of the trains penetrated my dreams. The sound of their clatter turned into shouts of rage in my fitful sleep, adding to my loneliness.

The sounds of the home coming to life woke me early the next morning. 'It's Christmas Day,' I said to myself when I opened my eyes. I reached for the two parcels. I opened the one from my aunt first and found inside a glass bottle of perfume with matching body lotion and soap. I sniffed it appreciatively, then put it to one side and pulled the bulkier package, the one that Dora had brought, onto the bed. It was a pair of brown leather boots lined with a soft fur; the nicest present I had ever been given. Tucked inside was a card with my mother's handwriting. 'To keep your feet warm when you come home,' she had written, and I knew those few words were her way of telling me that she understood a little of what I must be feeling. I put both presents in my locker, then dressed and went downstairs to join the other girls.

What I remember most about that day is the mothers gathered in the lounge with their babies on their knees as they pretended just for those few hours that we were a normal group of girls who were part of a large happy family. Maybe for that day we were; petty animosities were forgotten and pregnant girls cooed over tiny bundles held proudly in the arms of the new mothers. The matron presented each baby with a small fluffy toy. The radio was turned on to a carol service, and just for a few minutes the music lifted our spirits.

Later that day we had our Christmas dinner. While the meal was tasty, in fact better than we ever had at home, and everyone tried to be cheerful as they pulled crackers, read out the jokes and wore coloured paper hats, a slight sense of gloom seemed to hover over the long table of girls.

Helpless

We all knew that we were celebrating the birth of a baby, and for most of us this was a painful thought, for it only highlighted what we were all preparing ourselves to do – give up ours the moment they were six weeks old.

After lunch we listened to the Queen's speech on the radio, then as a treat the lounge's television was turned on. We watched a Bing Crosby film, *White Christmas*, and then before we knew it our Christmas was over.

The few Christmas cards that the girls had received and left on the mantelpiece all depicted scenes of trees and bushes turned white by the thick flakes of sparkling winter snow. Seeing them, I wondered what country the artist had come from. When I looked through the large windows, instead of a white wonderland we had lashing rain and blustery winds – weather that forced even the most adventurous of the girls to remain indoors.

But I was a country girl, used to walking to school whatever the elements, and I missed the fresh air on my face and the quiet of the countryside where seldom even a passing car disturbed the peace. After months of not being able to leave my parents' house I felt I was trapped again, but this time by the weather.

'Can I go out for a walk?' I asked the matron, only to be told that the rain had made the grass slippery, too dangerous for a girl whose baby was almost due.

Every morning I hoped that the wind had driven the clouds away and that a winter sun would cast its rays over the gardens. But every morning, when I saw the ashen sky and heard the sound of rain lashing against the panes, my hopes were dashed.

That last week, when my baby was getting ready for her entrance into the world and had dropped lower down in my womb, I felt heavy, clumsy even, and tiredness never seemed to leave me. My breasts hurt, my back ached and, as I walked, I felt my body sway sideways as it tried to balance my unaccustomed weight and extended shape.

But I was waiting for this baby with such longing that those feelings of discomfort were of little consequence. Since that first time when I had felt my baby kick she had become real to me, and during those final days of waiting all I could think of was that soon I was going to meet her. When I looked in the mirror and saw my cumbersome shape, part of me loved it for it was the baby growing healthily that had pushed my stomach out and distorted my once petite frame.

My baby, though, seemed reluctant to enter the world. She was late, and I had passed the date I had been told I was due to give birth on. It was then that I felt both the longing to have my body back and an ever-increasing fear of the actual birth.

I had listened to my mother's screams when she gave birth and heard married women's furtive whispers of inconceivable pain. I always wondered why this was a pain that seemed to be forgotten the moment they started getting broody for another baby.

To my amazement I found I missed my mother with such intensity that it hurt. I tried unsuccessfully to push away any thoughts of the man next door; not even a Christmas card, letter or just something to give me support had arrived from him. He was the reason, I knew, that I was estranged from my family, and I began to feel hatred towards him because of it.

My daughter arrived in the morning. Like my mother had thirteen years before, I woke to a damp bed and a gripping pain. Unlike my mother, however, there was no warm body, however grumpy, to nudge – just a bell above my bed to push and summon help. Nor did I have a reassuring midwife who told me not to worry, that she would take care of everything. Instead there was just a grim-faced matron who gave one look at me and had me wheeled into the delivery room.

There was pain, a lot of it, and screams that tore out of my throat as my muscles strained to help my baby enter the world. I dimly remember the feeling of her sliding out of me, hearing her cry, and then there was darkness and I slept.

It was late afternoon when my eyes opened. A nurse was sitting by my bed. She told me that because of my youth I had lost a lot of blood and that I had needed stitches. Then she told me what I already knew: I had given birth to a baby girl.

'I want to see her, please,' I said. She was brought to me – a tiny six-pound bundle. My arms went out and curled round her as she was placed in them. I cannot even now find the words to describe that sweeping love that I felt when I looked at her for the first time and inhaled her scent, the smell of newness.

One look at her tiny face, still red and scrunched up from the effort of her journey, her rounded limbs, that fuzz of dark-blonde hair and the utter helplessness of her, and I just wanted to hold her for ever. I searched her features carefully and could see nothing in them of the man next door. They were, I thought, simply miniature versions of my own.

The matron arrived and told me that I was very weak. 'You have to rest – you had a tough time, Marianne.'

I was incapable of protesting. I felt my baby being taken from my arms, my eyes drooped and the next thing I remember was the following morning.

The nurse helped me out of bed and took me to the nursery where she showed me how to bottle feed her and change her nappy; both I had already learnt to do at a much earlier age.

That first morning when I sat on a chair with her snuggled firmly in my arms, I was in a little world of my own, a world where only she and I existed. I crooned a song into her ear as I looked dreamily down at her. Her head rested against my chest and I marvelled at the strength of the tiny mouth sucking on the bottle's teat.

When she had taken her fill I placed her gently against my shoulder, inhaling as I did so that intoxicating perfume of a newborn – fresh skin, talcum powder and milk – and gently patted her back. A tiny fist rested on my shoulder, a soft burp fluttered against my cheek, a dribble of milk dampened my shoulder, warm gentle breath whispered in my ear; my baby had fallen asleep.

I kissed her again, placed her back in her cot and covered her small form with a crocheted blanket. Then I stayed by her side, content to watch her sleep until the nurse took me by the arm to lead me back to my bed.

My mother arrived and came and sat by my bed. 'Are you all right, Marianne?' she asked.

A stupid question, I thought, for how could I be all right when in six weeks' time my baby was going to be taken away?

I felt a dull resentment towards her then, for why could she not have welcomed my baby into the house? My father had let her stay when Jack was born, hadn't he? Round and round those thoughts circled in my head, making it impossible to talk to her.

She sensed that, sighed and rose to leave.

'I know what you are thinking,' she said, 'but believe me it's better this way. You've got your whole life in front of you, and one day you will get married have more children, but for now you are just too young.'

My eyes rested on her breasts, swollen with milk for my latest brother, and my resentment grew. I turned my face away to hide the tears, and without speaking again she left.

Chapter Thirty-four

Over those days when I stayed in the recovery room regaining my strength, I loved every moment that I had with my baby; loved that warm protective feeling that I felt when I fed, bathed and held her. I called her Sonia, the name I had chosen for her when I had first felt her move inside me and been convinced she was a girl. I just wished that I could have done all those nurturing things alone instead of under the watchful eye of either the matron or the nurse. If only it had been summer, I thought, I might have been allowed to wheel her outside in a pram and taken her to the large orchard behind the home. There I would have sat under one of the trees, its leaves sheltering her from the sun, and simply looked at her. But the winter days were too cold for a newborn to venture out, and instead I had to content myself with being with her within the four walls of the nursery.

She was such a sunny-natured baby who even from her first day in the world slept contentedly and seldom cried. That consoled me somehow, for if she had been a difficult child wouldn't it be harder for her new parents to love her?

Then I did what I always did when the words 'new parents' came into my head – I pushed them firmly away.

Once I had regained my strength I was allowed to move back to my room and Sonia's cot was placed beside my bed.

'Now, Marianne, make sure she sleeps in there,' the matron said, not without some sympathy. 'I know what you girls can be like, taking the babes into their beds. But it only makes things harder for you when the time comes.' I did not need to be reminded what time she was referring to.

Seeing that I did not want to understand the meaning behind her words she uncharacteristically sat on the end of my bed. 'Look, Marianne, I can see you are getting attached to her, and don't think I don't understand. It's nature's way. But you know that she is not going home with you, so don't make things more difficult for yourself. That's all the advice I can give you.' Then she rose from the bed, sighed and left me alone with my baby.

Of course I paid no attention to the matron's words, and every chance I had I cuddled Sonia, lay her beside me on the bed and listened to her breathing. I whispered and crooned to her and sang her little songs telling her of how much I loved her.

Our days together slipped by into weeks until I suddenly realized that the time for separation, that time that I had pushed all thought of to the back of my mind, was less than a few days away.

I was propelled into reality when the matron asked, 'Marianne, have you brought a special outfit for your baby to wear when she meets her new parents?'

I looked at her blankly for I had no money so how could I have bought my baby clothes?

'Don't worry,' matron said on seeing my crestfallen face, 'we will find her something pretty. They are going to love her anyhow, she's such a good little soul.'

Those days, those final days I had with her, I prayed and prayed that my parents would relent and let me take her home with me. She was so beautiful, so good that I knew she would not be a bother. Besides what real difference would one more baby in our house make? It didn't happen. There was no grandmother rushing in at the last minute to say she had changed her mind and that she wanted to take her new granddaughter home to be part of the family. The worst day of my life arrived.

That morning when I bathed and dried her, I stroked every inch of that perfect little body. I wanted the feel of her skin engraved in my memory. I gazed and gazed at her so that whenever I closed my eyes I would be able to bring her picture into my mind for I did not even have a photograph to take with me from the home. After I had fed her for the last time, the matron arrived and brought me the outfit I was to dress her in. It was a blue romper suit.

'Haven't you got a pink one?' I asked desperately. The thought of handing my daughter over dressed in a boy baby's clothes was unbearable. I thought the least I can do was make her look perfect. I wanted 'them' to see the care I had taken of her – know she was loved by me; for that was what I wanted them to tell my, our daughter one day.

'It's the only spare one we have,' the matron said. 'I'm sorry, Marianne, but she will have to wear it.' And I saw that she understood my desperate plea.

She put her hand gently on my shoulder.

'It won't matter to her new parents, Marianne. I told you, they are going to love her.'

But it mattered to me.

I tried not to cry. I did not want my daughter's last memories of me to be of my tears falling on her. The grief of losing her was frozen inside me; that I would look at later when I was able to. But the sorrow I felt when I thought that my baby was going to start her new life in that blue romper suit was almost unbearable.

My social worker arrived later that morning. It was her duty to take my baby to her new parents. I can't remember what she said when she took her from my arms. I only know that I stood trance-like by the window, watching my daughter being carried out and placed in the social worker's car.

That was my last memory of her before she disappeared from view: a tiny bundle dressed in those baby boy's clothes.

As she was driven away I imagined her fear of suddenly being taken from everything she knew, of being in that car with its strange smells and rocky movements.

Would she wonder where I was? I asked myself. Would she not want to feel my hands petting her and hear my voice telling her she was loved? Would she cry? I wondered. Would she meet her new parents with a tear-stained face?

The last question that spun round and round in my head then was: How long would it take her to forget me?

Chapter Thirty-five

It was my father, driving the man next door's car, who came to collect me that afternoon. That drive, what we spoke about, if indeed we spoke at all, remains just a blur. I must have said goodbye to someone, must have thanked the matron, but I have no recollection of it, nor can I remember any of the days spent at home before I started school again. My grief was overwhelming and I felt as if I was walking in a dream, one where you could feel nothing except loss and see nothing except my baby's face.

My mother would, I know, have taken me into town to purchase my school uniform. I know that it must have occurred because on the day I started at my new school it was hanging on the back of my bedroom door, ready for me to wear.

There was a grey skirt, a crisp white blouse and a blue blazer on the hook and on the floor was a pair of new black school shoes with new white socks tucked inside. This time, it seemed, my parents wanted me to look the same as the other girls.

My father, much to my surprise, drove me to the new school on my first day.

'You have to be there early,' he said by way of explanation, 'Your headmistress wants to meet you before school starts.'

I felt a wave of apprehension. Did she know about me? Know that I had been expelled from my former school nearly nine months ago? Even worse, had she been told why? I wanted to ask, to be reassured that she didn't know, but the words 'pregnant', 'baby' or 'adoption' and 'Marianne' were never mentioned in the same sentence by either of my parents. It was as if it had never happened.

The drive there was over all too quickly for me. Without saying a word of encouragement my father just pulled up in front of the school gates and waited for me to alight. Feeling my legs shake with nerves as I placed them on the ground, I climbed out.

The school was bigger than my previous one and I could see tennis courts and green lawns, but nothing succeeded in distracting me from that sick feeling of apprehension that was fluttering in my stomach. I slung my satchel over my shoulder and walked reluctantly into the school, seeking out the headmistress's study.

To my relief, instead of the stern forbidding woman of my imagination, a smiling small plump one greeted me and ushered me inside. She made it clear that, although she knew about my pregnancy, she was not going to judge me.

'Hallo, Marianne, come and sit down,' were the first words she said to me, followed by, 'You have been through a terrible time, I know, but I hope you will be happy here.' At her unexpected kindness the tears I had refused to shed since I had returned home threatened to overspill my smarting eyes, but the headmistress tactfully ignored my obviously emotional state.

'Now is the time to look at your future, Marianne,' she told me, before asking if I had thought what I wanted to do when I reached the school-leaving age of fifteen. I saw that lying on her desk in clear view of me were my files from my old school and knew that they would contain my reports and all the notes regarding my expulsion.

I had never dreamed of a career, but suddenly for the first time I realized what it was that I really wanted to do – to train as a children's nurse.

I blurted out my ambition to her and waited for her to tell me what I already knew – that my grades were not good and that I had lost too much time at school. Instead she heard me out without interrupting and smiled encouragingly at me.

She did tell me that my schoolwork would need to be improved but she saw no reason why, if I worked hard, that could not be done. Instead she explained that it might just be possible for me to go to a teaching hospital where I would live in the nurses' home and start training as an auxiliary nurse. From there with a lot of hard work and practical experience I might progress up the nursing ladder. She explained that whilst academic qualifications helped you qualify faster there was another route for girls like me.

For the first few weeks I was at my new school I worried that someone other than the headmistress might know about my past. I dreaded being asked questions about where I had been at school before and why I had left it, but to my relief no one seemed curious about me.

Gradually I relaxed; the smart uniform, which helped me blend in with the other scholars, gave me more confidence than I had previously had. I began to work harder because for the first time I had a goal that could only be achieved by raising my grades. I started talking to the other girls about their ambitions and some of them wanted to go to college but most were just looking forward to the independence that earning a wage would give them.

They wanted not to have to do homework or study but be able to buy make-up and clothes, find a boyfriend and stay at home until they got married. Unlike them I knew that I wanted to leave my parents' home as soon as it was possible and also do something worthwhile with my life. To spend those years it took to train as a nurse and get my feet firmly on the career ladder was my driving ambition. I still missed my baby, but that was a dull ache that I tucked away at the back of my mind and avoided examining, as it was still too painful.

There was one other girl who also wanted to become a nurse. 'Might meet a good-looking doctor,' she said with a grin. 'That's first prize, but nurses also marry policemen and firemen, that's what my mum says.' I found myself smiling back, not because I shared that dream, but for the first time I felt I was making a friend of my own.

She told me that her name was Susan, that she had a younger sister but had always wished she had a brother. She said I was lucky to have three brothers and a sister. Lucky? That was not something I had ever thought of before. Never having a moment's peace, always surrounded by noise and mess, endless chores and intrusion was what having siblings meant to me.

Susan, with her long blonde hair and tall slim frame, looked exactly how I, at only four foot eleven, wanted to look. Boys' eyes followed her wherever she walked but she just tossed her hair and showed them little interest. She dismissed them, saying she did not see those sorts of boys ever becoming doctors. Other girls wanted her as their friend but it was me she had singled out. We started sitting together in class, standing next to each other in assembly and in the playground, and eating our school dinners together at the same table.

She even walked with me to my bus stop before continuing on foot to her own home, and then after a few weeks she invited me to her house for tea.

'Come tomorrow,' she said. 'I told my mother I had made friends with a girl in my class and she said I could bring you home.'

'My first invitation to tea!' I thought, and some of the grief I had carried around deep inside of me shifted.

'Do you like that new group, the Beatles?' she asked and, wanting to be accepted, I nodded my head enthusiastically, even though I had never heard of them or their music.

'Good. I've just got their single, "Please Please Me". We can listen to it in my room after tea.'

'I'll be out for tea,' I told my mother casually the next morning.

She looked doubtfully at me.

'It's Susan, you know, the girl I told you about. She's invited me to her house.'

'All right,' my mother said, 'just don't be late home. And not a minute after seven thirty – you still have your homework to do. And don't miss that last bus.'

That day I felt a little bubble of excitement rising up inside me. Finally I had made a friend in my own age group. The moment the school bell rang and announced lessons were finished, I picked up my satchel and followed Susan out of the classroom.

Her home, a semi-detached house with bay windows and a solid wooden front door, was within walking distance. Twenty minutes later I was standing in her sitting room being introduced to her mother as Marianne, the new girl at school.

It was when we were sitting down for tea that I knew something was wrong.

Susan's mother asked me what my father did for a living and I could tell that my reply that he worked on a farm was not met with approval, even though her smile remained on her face; a smile that slipped off it when I answered her next question.

'Where do you live, Marianne?' she had asked. Thrown, I gave her the name of the road, hoping that she knew nobody in it. My wish was not to be granted. 'What's your surname?' she asked slowly and, with a sinking feeling, I told her.

The plate of food that she was in the middle of passing to me landed on the table with a bang. 'Susan,' she said to her daughter, 'come into the kitchen – now!' and with a bewildered look my new friend obeyed.

Her younger sister looked goggle-eyed at me. She had sensed the atmosphere in the room change and knew it was something I had said that had caused it. I just sat on the chair wanting to leave.

Through the door I heard the faint words including 'slut', 'not in my house' and 'don't want you mixing with the likes of her', and pushing my plate aside I picked up my satchel, walked into the hall, opened the front door as quietly as I could and crept away.

Susan ran after me and walked with me as far as the bus stop. She tried to apologize for her mother's outburst and said that she was still my friend.

'You won't be tomorrow,' I thought, and I was right.

It turned out that Susan's mother knew Dora, who had given her a distorted version of what had happened.

She had only been good to me, and how had I repaid her? I had slept with her husband, become pregnant by him and had the baby adopted.

When Susan's mother had told her daughter Dora's version of the facts there was no need for her mother to forbid her to mix with me; that was a decision she came to all by herself. What was even worse than the loss of her friendship was her telling everyone in our class why she no longer wanted to speak to me.

In the classroom she changed seats, leaving me sitting alone. I tried to talk to her in the playground but she gave me a look that held both contempt and pity.

'My mother says you are a cheap little whore,' she said, loud enough for the girls nearby to hear, 'and that I'm not to mix with you.' Then, linking arms with a mousy-haired sycophantic girl, she walked away. Her latest best friend threw me a triumphant look and I heard them laugh. My face burnt with shame for I knew that I was the object of their merriment and I wanted the ground to open up and swallow me.

All that week I was aware of girls huddling in groups as they whispered about the scandal, while boys made sniggering lewd remarks.

'Hey, Marianne,' one swaggering teenager, bolder than the rest, called out to me, 'what's it feel like having a baby wriggling around inside you?'

'Something else wriggled in you first, though, didn't it?' said another, and the group collapsed with laughter.

It took six months for them to get bored with baiting me: six months where I held my head up as I tried to ignore both the malicious innuendo and the spiteful titters; six months when every night I cried into my pillow. I had so hoped I would fit in, but again I was alone.

Chapter Thirty-six

No sooner had my new, happier life at school crumbled away than the truce between my father and me ended. Since experiencing the rigorous routine at the girls' home I had become what my parents considered to be obsessively tidy. At weekends when I looked at the dirty surfaces, piles of unwashed dishes and the bucket full with the newest baby's dirty nappies, it made my nose wrinkle in distaste and I decided to do something about it.

One Saturday, as soon as my mother had gone to the shops, taking the youngest child with her, and my father had left for work, I sent my brothers and sister out in the garden to play, rolled up my sleeves and scrubbed and cleaned.

Not only did I like making the house look as nice as possible, but also keeping busy stopped me dwelling on Susan and the looks of contempt that came my way whenever I saw her.

First the nappies were put into the largest saucepan and boiled, then I tackled the stack of washing up, wiped every spot of grease off the work surfaces and finally got down on my hands and knees to clean the floor. By the time my mother returned the kitchen was gleaming; a state that never lasted long. By the following weekend the floor was littered with crumbs, congealed food had yet again stuck to the table and oven and the pile of grubby nappies was back in the bucket. Every Saturday I simply started all over again.

As I worked, I let my mind wander to the life I was going to have once I left school. I dreamt of leaving home, of going to train as a nurse and of wearing that smart starched blue and white uniform. Emptying bedpans and scrubbing floors, however, was never part of that dream. Instead I pictured small faces turned trustingly up to me and grateful parents saying how thankful they were that it was me who had looked after their child.

Oh, how different my life was going to be then, I thought as I cleaned and polished. In the nurse's home, instead of having to share with my sister, who left her toys strewn around our bedroom, I would have a room of my own. On my bed there would be clean crisp sheets and wool blankets instead of those old clothes that served to keep us warm. My clothes would be hung up neatly, my undies would be new and clean, and best of all no little fingers would touch my toiletries.

It was those thoughts that gave me hope, and it was that hope that made me work at my studies. In the evenings my school books would be spread on the kitchen table as I worked hard to catch up with my peers; something that my father sneered at, but not as much as he did at my cleaning the house.

If I had thought my parents would be pleased by my domesticated efforts I was wrong. Instead they seemed almost affronted, as though every time I picked up a brush or mop it was a criticism of the way they lived.

'Think you're too good for us now,' my father said with a snort when he saw me ironing my school uniform. 'Proper little madam you've become.' I just looked at him and ignored what he said, but that did not stop the disloyal thoughts running through my head.

'If you want to live like pigs, I don't,' I longed to say, but commonsense made me refrain from voicing those words. Maybe something in my expression told him what was in my mind, for his torrent of sneering comments at my efforts increased.

'See you've even been scrubbing our lav,' he said derisively. When going to the outside lavatory he had found it not just scrubbed clean but smelling of disinfectant. 'You'll be wanting to scrub us all next.'

'Oh, don't take any notice of him, Marianne,' my mother said wearily when he had stomped out after one of his outbursts; but I noticed that she did not thank me either.

It only took a few weeks for my father to show me even more clearly what he thought of my efforts at making our home nicer. I was on my hands and knees scrubbing the floor when he came back from work early. That morning, intent on getting to the back yard, he walked across the room with his muddy boots, leaving a trail of dirt in his wake.

It was too much for me to keep silent. I stood up and glared at him.

'Please, Dad,' I said, 'I've spent an hour cleaning that floor. Won't you take your boots off?'

His face turned red with rage. Just for those few moments I had forgotten how quickly my father's temper could erupt.

'Who do you think you are? Think you can give me orders, do you?' Seeing his face and his raised arm I shrunk back in fear, but not fast enough. The blow hit me on my shoulder so hard that I lost my balance and slipped and fell onto the still wet floor. At the same time his foot struck the bucket, sending sheets of dirty water across the kitchen.

'Well, you can clean it again,' he yelled. 'Seems that's what you like doing the most.' I hated him then, and, sniffling with both hurt and shock, I got down on my hands and knees to wipe up the mess he had made.

Once finished I went to my room. 'Let the children fend for themselves for once,' I thought as I lay on my bed. There I took refuge in my dreams of leaving home, escaping a family that day by day I felt I was ceasing to belong to and not having to hear the cruel sniggers at school. I wanted to go to where no one knew me, no one knew my parents and no one knew about my baby.

Chapter Thirty-seven

Looking back on that day as I sat looking at my small pile of photographs and the envelope, I felt the futile need to pick up the phone and speak to my own mother. I wanted answers to some of the same questions I felt my daughter wanted from me.

Did you ever love me, Mother? When you carried me, did you want me? Or was I just the reason you got married?

And the one question I wanted the answer to more than any other: Even if you didn't, even if you felt nothing when you first held me, did you grow to care for me, your eldest daughter? I know you loved my brothers and sister, but did you ever love me?

Those questions that had so often screamed out silently in my head, those questions that I had never found the courage to voice, were once again in my mind.

But I had left them too late to ask, for several years previously my mother had passed the stage of remembering my childhood.

I pictured her hunched form and vacant stare as, locked into her own world, she looked uncomprehendingly at me.

I was no longer even a trace in my mother's mind: dementia had mercifully taken away her memories of a life which had known little happiness. Except for one: that of her husband.

'Oh, but he was handsome,' she would say with a sigh as his face drifted through the fog she lived in. 'Oh, but he was such a handsome man.' And that one sentiment told me why she had stayed all those years. And I would smile at her, tuck a blanket around her age-withered knees, pat a trembling shoulder, brush sparse hair or gently stroke her face; anything to show that the residue of my childhood love still remained.

When I reached adulthood and was myself married I had forgiven my mother for her lack of care. With the understanding that maturity brings, as opposed to the feelings of the angry, hurt, neglected child, I had seen the sadness not just in my life but in hers as well.

Practically my mother's entire ration of love had been used up on her husband. A small portion of it had been shared between the children she wanted, but there had been little over for me and even less for herself.

My thoughts drifted to dwell fleetingly on my father, who withered by age and alcohol abuse had died several years before my mother's dementia had placed her in the nursing home. I remembered his tempers, his violence and the very occasional moment that showed me that once someone nicer had lived within his mind.

No, my questions of them had been left too late to ask, but my daughter's hadn't and I was going to have to answer them.

I cast my mind back to those years and asked myself if there was anything I could have done differently. If I had known what I do now I suppose I could have, but I didn't. And if I had – I said to the letter – then you would not have written to me for you would not have been born.

I thought of that lie I had told to the social worker and the matron; that lie which at thirteen had set the course for what was to follow.

Even then, nearly a quarter of a century later, I still could not accept those years when I had conceived not just one but two daughters, carried them for nine months, loved them even before they entered the world, then when they were still tiny babies handed them both over for adoption.

There were so many nights when those images of another time had visited me. My sleep set them free to roam in my dreams and so often when I awoke they demanded to be remembered; something that I tried so often to deny them.

Chapter Thirty-eight

By the time I had settled back at home, the man next door seemed to have taken on the appearance of a phantom presence. There was only the odd glimpse of the back of his head or a quick view of his profile as he stepped from his car. Before my eyes had focused or my lips had time to call his name he had disappeared so quickly that I was left wondering if it was my imagination that had conjured him up.

Sometimes I heard his children calling 'Daddy' and occasionally I saw Dora peering through her window, watching for him to arrive, and just once I thought I saw him in the street. I quickened my pace that day but when I closed the gap between us it was only to see a stranger. Apart from that he seemed to have disappeared from my life. But I was relieved, wasn't I? I no longer liked him, did I? But still I wondered, just sometimes, if he ever thought of me.

It was four o'clock in the afternoon when that questioned was answered. I was at the bus stop when I heard the sound of a car slowing down.

'Hello, little lady,' said a voice from inside it and, turning, I looked into the face of the man next door.

To my amazement he leant over and opened the passenger door. 'Get in,' he said. I looked at him incredulously as the hurt of months welled up inside me, and then I turned and walked off.

He followed me.

'Go away,' I said. 'I don't want to talk to you.'

'But I have something to say to you,' he replied, giving me what he thought was a winning smile. 'Come on, get inside.'

That time I didn't, nor did I the next day or the one after that.

But the fourth time I did.

'I'm so sorry,' he said. 'I didn't have a choice; but I thought of you often.' I tried not to listen to him, but as these sentiments, the ones that I so wanted to hear, started to pour out from him, just for a short time that first day, I believed him. Memories of how he had been when I had first met him – when he had listened to my stories and made me feel special – superimposed themselves over the more recent painful ones. That day, when he spoke to me for the first time after so many months, those other memories, of his blackmailing threats and cruelty, were, if not forgotten, then pushed temporarily to the recesses of my mind.

He gave me a present, a beautiful silver locket. 'Wear it under your blouse,' he said.

And then slowly, every time after that when he and I met, little by little the mistrust of the recent years slipped away until once again he seemed my childhood friend, the one to whom I could tell my dreams and fears.

He listened to me and, unlike my parents, showed interest in everything I said. His face showed concern when I repeated what Susan and her mother had called me. His arm went briefly around my shoulder when I confided in him how different I felt from my family and how much the latest row with my father had upset me. But I never talked about the girls' home or our baby, and he never asked me.

I told him about my ambition to train as a nurse; how I could not wait for the months to pass until I could.

'I'll miss you, Marianne,' he said. I thought then that he was the only person who would. But later, when I was alone and free of his power over me, I again remembered how he had been and how he had deserted me when I became pregnant.

'You lied to me,' I said once. 'Girls don't get hung for having sex with men. They told me in the home.'

He told me that he had only said that for my sake. Surely I knew that there was more than one sort of trouble that I could have brought down on myself if I had talked? Hadn't I found that out already?

I had; it meant no one talked to me. They just talked about me.

I was still naïve enough to believe him, because I wanted to, and I gave little thought to the fact it would have been him who would have been in deeper trouble.

I did not recognize that the man next door had started his wooing of me all over again; that his was a game of patience and skill, honed sharply by his intimate knowledge of me and all my youthful weaknesses. He knew of my loneliness, my feelings of isolation at home and at school. For hadn't I told him all about it myself? I did not know then that each time I laid bare a little piece of my soul I handed him the tools to control me again.

The first part of his game was to make me pleased to see him. That was a simple one – some days he arrived, other days he didn't. And after a short time I started looking for his car as, of course, he had known I would. The second part was not difficult either – making me believe that he was the only person who cared for me, a sentiment that he cleverly reinforced each time we met. He never tried to touch me, not then. Gradually I began to trust him again while he prepared for the final part of his game.

Chapter Thirty-nine

I finally turned fifteen – the birthday I had been looking forward to, for that was the age of freedom. What I overlooked was that, although I was old enough to leave school and work by law, I needed my parents' permission to live anywhere else but their home.

A few days before that birthday, the one I considered such a milestone in my life, the headmistress called me into her study. She told me that it looked as though my ambition was going to be possible. A hospital in the north of England had agreed that I could start on their training programme. There I could live in, and although my wages would be minimal, the hospital would provide my board and keep. The best part, although the head-mistress did not spell it out in so many words, was that none of the girls at my school had applied to go there. That, combined with the fact that the hospital was so far away from my home, made it very unlikely that I would bump into anyone who knew me.

'It will be a fresh start for you, Marianne, and you deserve that,' she said gently. 'You have worked very hard this year to get your grades up. I'm very pleased for you.' I recognized by the expression on her face that, even though she knew little about my home life, she had known how the other pupils had ostracized and victimized me.

Her next sentence, though, suddenly brought me face to face with the reality of what this job offer meant.

'Your parents will have to write a letter giving their permission for you to go.'

'What happens if they don't?' was my next timorous question.

'Why, Marianne, without it the hospital would not take you. Surely you have discussed this whole idea with your family?'

'Oh! Yes, of course,' I lied.

I waited until suppertime to tell my parents.

'What? You went behind our backs and arranged this?' said my furious father. 'You thought you could do that without talking to your mum or me? I suppose we don't count? We're just the people who feed and clothe you, are we? Well, if you think I'm giving my permission for this nonsense, you can think again.'

My mother examined her hands intently and twisted her thin wedding ring and said nothing.

'Time you put some money back into this house, my girl!' he continued. 'You'll get a job round here and start paying for your keep. Show a bit of gratitude for everything we've done for you. Everything we've had to put up with. It's the least you can do.'

I tried pointing out that they would not have to feed me if I was not at home, but he refused to listen.

I pleaded, I cried. But it was no use. I turned to my mother for support. 'No point looking at her, Marianne – your mum agrees with me. Don't you?' he said, turning in her direction with such a ferocious look that I knew she would be too scared to argue.

'You can't go unless we write a letter saying it's all right with us for you to leave home. Isn't that true?' I gave a miserable nod. 'Well, I'm not going to do it. No chance!' he said with a note of triumph in his voice.

He paused for a moment to ram another fork of food into his mouth, then he looked up at my stunned and unhappy face again. 'You know what you are going to do tomorrow? You're going to get a job in that new factory. There's a sign up saying they want workers. They pay good money, they do. So you mind you get yourself down there. Now I don't want to hear another word.'

Before I could open my mouth to protest one more time he aimed his final verbal shot at me. 'Anyway, Marianne, you've given us enough trouble. You'll not be leaving home at fifteen and getting yourself into any more.'

I did not return to school the next morning. Instead I went to the factory and asked to see the person who was interviewing all the school leavers. I was told to report for work the following Monday. They would train me to be a coil winder.

My father was right. They did pay well.

But no amount of money could compensate me for my shattered dreams.

Chapter Forty

When here I was working was a large modern building on an industrial estate, one of the many that were being constructed in our area. My supervisor, a slight, mousy-haired man wearing wire-framed glasses, explained, in his strong London accent, what would be expected of me.

The following Monday morning I was to come to his office at seven forty-five where he would show me the room where my initial two-week training course was to take place. I was going to learn how to do coil winding for the growing telecommunications industry. I would be taught how to use a soldering iron and to recognize the different gauges of wires that I would be working with. As I racked my brains about what I would wear, all I could settle on was my school-uniform skirt and a hand-knitted jumper from the second-hand shop. I had washed and pressed each item the night before so, even if it looked old fashioned and childlike, at least my attire was clean. When I nervously reported for work I found myself with a group of older women who were also starting at the factory that day. We were taken to a small outer building where, after a few minutes of introductions, we started our first lesson. To my surprise, although I found the work both boring and tedious I also found it easy because of my small hands. Praise rained down on me that first day, and suddenly working in the factory did not seem as bad as I had thought it was going to be.

I was the youngest by at least five years. Most of the other women had husbands who also worked in one of the nearby factories. Some of them had moved from inner London, seduced by better schools for their children and the opportunity to buy an affordable semi-detached house on one of the new estates that were beginning to cover the Essex landscape. They were a friendly bunch, and when the factory whistle blew to tell us we had a fifteen-minute break for tea, I found myself sitting with a couple of women who seemed determined to take me under their wing as they had worked there for some time.

'You're a little one, aren't you! How long since you left school, love?' said one, a dark-haired woman with smiling brown eyes and a smattering of freckles over her snub nose, who told me her name was Bev.

'Only just left,' I replied, feeling then the stab of sharp disappointment at not being on my way to the nurse's home.

Her friend, whose name was Jean, said, 'Well, that explains your clothes,' but her tone was not unkindly.

I wriggled a bit then. I was only too aware that they, with their permed hair and made-up faces, presented a very different image than I, with my hair tied neatly back and my face devoid of any make-up whatsoever. Even though we all wore some sort of protective clothing, I could see that both Bev and Jean were wearing outfits that were nicer than anything I had in my meagre wardrobe. My heart sank once again and I felt that I was never going to fit in. Apart from my school uniform, all I had were a few second-hand dresses that, because I was so small, were either too young or too large for me.

I knew the cost of clothes. I had looked into enough shop windows with a longing for something new and fashionable, but I knew it would take me a long time to save up for anything like the outfits my fellow workers were wearing. My father had told me how much I was expected to give my mother each week for my board and keep and, having learnt what my wage would be, I knew it left very little over for me.

'Tell you what, love,' Bev said, on seeing my downcast face. 'I make most of my own clothes – got an electric sewing machine at my house. I'll run you up couple of pretty outfits, no problem. All you need to do is find the material.'

Before I could ask her if she really meant it, she continued as though what she was suggesting was an everyday occurrence in my life.

'We can go shopping when you get your first pay packet Friday week. Now, I want to do a bit of overtime on Saturday. You can put your name down for that too as soon as you've finished your training. Then we'll pop into town to that new store that's just opened and buy some pretty fabric.'

'I've got to give most of my wages to my mother,' I told her. 'There's another four younger than me at home that need feeding.'

'Don't worry,' she said. 'It won't cost much – it will only take a couple of yards to cover your tiny figure. Tell you what, you can stay and have a bite to eat at my house and I'll get it cut out, then my hubby and me will drive you home.'

I was not to know that day as I mumbled my grateful thanks that this was the start of a friendship which, in the months that followed, would prove to be one of the most important of my life.

My first pay packet was handed to me on the Friday afternoon. It was a sealed brown envelope with the calculation of my wages written on the outside. It stated how many hours I had worked and how much was inside. I took it home and gave it to my mother, still unopened. From it she removed a note and some coins; the latter she handed back to me.

'That's for you, Marianne,' she told me. 'You spend it on something you want.' Furthermore, when I told her about the possibility of earning overtime, she said that I could keep that extra money. I found my face breaking into a smile as I wondered if I was going to have enough money to go shopping after all.

That Saturday afternoon I went into town with Bev and searched the shops that were selling dress fabric. I found a small remnant of pastel material dotted with sprigs of tiny flowers that Bev said she could turn into a blouse. She then found quite a reasonably sized piece of navy-blue fabric to make me a flared skirt, one that was nipped in at the waist and would swirl around my knees as I walked. 'It'll show off that tiny waist of yours,' she said with a smile, and happily I agreed. My meagre allowance just covered these purchases and I could barely contain my excitement. We celebrated with tea and a cream cake before we went home. 'My treat!' said Bev. 'You can do the next time when you get your first overtime.'

A couple of hours later I was in my new friend's house being measured from every angle so she could get the cut right. When I had first walked in I instantly loved her house and admired its new three-piece draylon suite, fitted floral carpet and shiny pale-teak dining table and chairs. In comparison, my parents' home looked even shabbier.

'Lovely, aren't it, Marianne? The coffee table's my favourite, though it's that Ercol! Cost a bomb, but it's quality. Got it all on the never-never,' Bev told me. 'Wanted to get everything new before we start a family.'

Her husband, a chunky blond-haired man in his late twenties, worked in another factory doing piecework, which paid even better money than we were on.

Within a short time I found myself eating once a week with Bev and her husband, and then afterwards they drove me home. That first time, as their car turned into the lane where I lived, I was aware of how our house, with its thin ill-fitting curtains hanging in the windows and the peeling paint on the front door, must have looked to them. But whatever they thought, they did not say anything; they just dropped me off and wished me good night.

Theirs was the first relationship I had seen of what is now termed a modern marriage. They both worked and earned money and they jointly decided how it was spent. They also went out together in the evenings, first discussing what they wanted to do. Sometimes they went to a cinema or the pub, and once a month they dressed up and went out for a meal and then dancing. On Sundays, though, Bev always cooked a roast dinner while Phil washed the car and worked in the garden. It was Phil's job to wash up the dishes afterwards, and then they watched television and just lazed around together. I had never heard of a man helping with housework, and it was also my first glimpse at what a happy marriage could be like.

The only thing missing, Bev confided to me, was a baby. The hire purchase was all paid off and Phil was due promotion to a better job as a supervisor. That meant that Bev had no real necessity to work, and they both felt it was the right time to start a family. They had been trying, but so far without success she told me, and a sad expression came into her eyes. Those words made me feel even guiltier, for what would she think if she knew not only had I had a baby, but that I had given her away?

It was during those early weeks of knowing them that I allowed the thought to enter my head that maybe, just maybe, I might meet someone nice; someone I too could marry and settle down with one day. But no sooner did that idea enter my head than I banished it. Men, I had been told, like their wives to have been good before they met them, and who decent would accept my past?

How could I ever tell anyone that not only was I not a virgin but that I had not been one since I was eight years old?

Chapter Forty-one

The day after I had been accepted at the factory I had gone to the school and told my headmistress of my father's decision. She had uttered conciliatory noises such as 'maybe when you are a little older', but she and I both knew that it was not going to happen. Once in a factory, girls rarely went back to study further and get qualifications. I could see in her eyes that these were hollow words of encouragement. I hated letting her down, and I hated my father's ignorance and his bullish refusal to help me improve my prospects.

It was that very day that the man next door appeared out of nowhere and listened to me when I tearfully told him that my father had refused to let me leave home and live in the nurses' home.

He had sympathized with my not being able to fulfil my ambition, and even confided in me that something similar had happened to him. He told me that he had wanted to stay on at school, pass exams and go on to university, but instead his father had insisted he learn a trade.

'Book learning doesn't pay a decent wage,' were his father's actual words, the man next door explained and, seeing the similarities in our shattered dreams, I believed him. Once he had finished his apprenticeship he met Dora, 'and then it was too late,' he added.

Later I wondered if even that was true or was it just another ruse to win my sympathy and make me feel we had a bond?

Several weeks passed before I saw him again, and in that time I had come, if not to like the routine of the factory, at least to get used to it. I enjoyed my growing friendship with Bev and the teasing I got from the other women as my appearance changed. With my overtime money I bought new underwear and shoes, had my hair cut and experimented with make-up for the first time. The real difference came when I started wearing the new outfits that Bev made for me at work.

'Don't keep it for best,' she had said after the first one was finished. 'I'll make you another one just as soon as you buy the fabric.'

It was a Saturday when the man next door put in another appearance. I had done a morning's overtime and was just leaving work when I heard his voice. This time he had walked up behind me.

'You look very pretty today, little lady.'

That day I was angry with him. Where had he been? Just turning up when he wanted to. He, seeing the expression on my face and understanding only too well the mixture of emotions running through my head, laughed.

'Missed me, did you?'

'No!' I replied a bit too quickly. 'Of course not.' But whether I admitted it or not, he knew I had.

'Heard you've been making plenty of new friends,' he said, and I supposed my mother had told Dora, who in turn had told him. Or perhaps he had been the one peeking through the curtains when Bev and Phil were dropping me off.

'You'll be forgetting me soon, won't you?' he said, looking defiantly into my eyes.

He received the answer he wanted: my denial.

He took my elbow and steered me in the direction of his car. With a flourish he flung open the passenger door and I climbed in. That time, instead of taking me straight home, the car turned off the road and into the woods.

He held his arms out to me. 'Come here, Marianne,' he said, and I flinched. He had spoilt the day. It made me realize just how I did not want to return to the situation of him making me do things that not only did I not like, but knew were wrong.

I cried a little, he stroked my back. I said I only wanted to talk.

'And this?' he said, his arm around my shoulder as his fingers gently stroked my neck. 'But you like this, don't you, Marianne?'

He was right. I did. I liked the comfort of being held. After all, he was still the only person who showed me affection. Ever since I was small and had seen parental affection only given to my younger siblings, I had wanted that intimacy for myself. But I did not want the other part of it, the part I knew he wanted.

For three weeks I said no to any other advances.

'Who did you say the father was?' he asked, a question that he must have been fully aware of the answer to.

'You know I told them I didn't know,' was my reply, hoping that he would show some gratitude for my protection of him.

'So,' he asked, 'when you filled in those forms, those official legal forms, about getting your baby adopted, what did you write on them? Also "father unknown"?'

'Yes,' I replied, emphatic that I had not betrayed him.

He explained to me then that what I had done was illegal. I had lied on a government form. His face was sombre and serious. 'Don't you know how serious that is, Marianne?'

'But you told me not to tell,' I said indignantly but with a creeping fear of having done something illegal.

I knew then that I had not given him the right answer, but what I did not know was that there was no right answer I could have given.

'I didn't tell you to lie on a government form!' was the terse response that he spat out at me.

I burst into tears at the unfairness of what he was saying.

Once again he said he would not let anything happen to me. His voice mellowed and he crooned in my ear and said he would do that because I was special to him. Once again I felt trapped and powerless to walk away from him.

That was the afternoon I didn't say no.

I swallowed my shame, for I still needed to hear those words telling me I was special.

He knew which words to use to manipulate me. He understood my fears and vulnerability, for had I not confided them all to him voluntarily?

Why did I let him abuse me again? That's a question I've asked myself over and over again. I did not love him; if anything I was scared of him. I hated what he did to me. But I was also scared of him not liking me. And I knew that he was stronger than me, more determined that he would make me give in than I was at refusing him. I felt that I had no choice.

I did not understand then that the real reason I went with him was because, at fifteen, I was still little more than a child, a child who from birth had been both lonely and emotionally deprived.

He was careful this time, careful not to be seen with me. He never came to our house or laid in wait for me near home. He just turned up on that stretch of road somewhere between the factory and the bus stop, turned up with that friendly smile and the right words to make me feel that someone cared, someone listened to me.

It was when I threw up one morning that I realized that he had not been as careful as he thought.

Chapter Forty-two

I waited a few days hoping against hope that my vomiting had been caused by something I had eaten. After three more days of throwing up before breakfast I had to face the fact that it wasn't, and with a sinking feeling I had to face the fact that it was three months since my last period. Surely this time he would have to help me? For the first time in several years it was me who went in search of him.

When I was certain there was no one around, I went to his workshop and left a note there for him saying that I had to see him.

The next day he was waiting for me near the factory and, as I climbed into his car, I blurted out that not only were my periods late, but I was also being sick every morning. 'Shit,' was the first word he said, followed by the same question he had asked me two years earlier: 'Are you sure it's mine?' I cried then, both in anger at his doubt and terror for the predicament I was in.

'I just can't go through that again,' I told him.

'Don't worry,' he said. 'You won't have to.' Then his arm went round my shoulders. But that day, instead of feeling comforting, its heaviness turned into a weight that seemed to press me down and trap me in my seat.

He told me that he would think of something and that he would be waiting for me when I finished work the following day.

That day dragged like no other, and when the clocking-off whistle blew, instead of hanging around for a chat with Bev, I just said a muttered goodbye, picked up my bag and left. His car drew up alongside before I had taken more than a few steps in the direction of the bus stop and his voice ordered me to jump in quickly. I knew immediately that this urgency was because he was scared that someone would see us together.

Into those woods we went, this time further in than he had ever driven before.

Grim faced, he reached into the back and brought out a bag which contained a flask and those coils of black rubber things I had last seen on the tray that Dora had held in her hands nearly two years earlier.

'No!' I screamed and tried to get out of the car. But he was too strong for me, his arm shot out and pushed me firmly down on the car's bench seat with one arm underneath me. Then before I could squirm away from him, he straddled me, one knee pinning me down and the other leg holding me in place against the car seat. He was stronger than me and I was terrified that he was really going to hurt me.

My knickers were pulled down to my ankles and my knees were pushed roughly apart and I felt the hard rubber of the nozzle being thrust inside me. I cried out in pain, for in his desperation and anger he was rougher than Dora had been and the soapy water in the flask was even hotter than I remembered. I thumped his shoulders and sobbed in fear as he poured it into me, but not until every drop was inside me did he pause. Then he climbed off me, pushed my legs together and jerked them roughly into the air.

'Got to keep that inside you for a bit,' he said. 'You want to get rid of it, Marianne, don't you? Think what your dad might do to you if he finds out this time.' And that thought made me shake with fear.

That afternoon the pain was far worse than I had remembered it being before. By the time I reached the part of the lane near our house where he always dropped me off, cramping pains and waves of nausea were making me feel faint and dizzy. Not wanting to arouse my mother's suspicions, I feigned a headache to give me an excuse to go straight upstairs to bed.

I tried to stop my moans of pain by stuffing the sheet in my mouth and chewed on it. I was frightened that my sister might hear me and tell my parents. Sweat beaded my forehead, pain shot through my body, and when tired-ness sent me into a merciful deep sleep I dreamed of a large pool of blood with a dead baby floating in it.

In the morning there was no sign of my period; instead I was sick again.

It was a week before the man next door turned up again.

'Well?' he said, when I climbed into the car.

'No sign,' I replied. Tears rolled down my cheeks as I described how I was still being sick every morning. With every word I uttered I saw all signs of my childhood friend disappear, until a stranger was sitting next to me, a stranger who looked at me with cold, angry eyes.

'You'd better stick to the same story as before,' he said eventually. 'Don't think you can drop me in it. Nobody would believe you.'

Oh, I tried to protest. I told him that he could not abandon me this time, that he had to help me, but he simply brushed aside my feeble efforts to get his support.

'Don't be a silly girl, Marianne,' he said, when I paused to draw breath. 'I'm a respectable married man. Ask anyone. While you? Didn't you go and tell the world that you were sleeping around when you were only thirteen? Didn't you write down on a government form that you didn't know who the father of your last baby was? Who's going to believe your lies now?'

Still I continued to beg him, and those pleas for help were met with a derisory laugh.

'If you mean help get you an abortion, forget it. They cost money and I haven't got any to spare. Anyhow, it's illegal. No, you just stick to that same old story. You should have got it off pat by now.'

He said nothing more, just drove until we were about a mile from our houses and then drew up.

For a moment I thought he must have had a change of heart or perhaps he had come up with an idea for helping me, but that hope was quickly dashed.

He just leant over me and opened the door.

'Get out, Marianne,' he said coldly. 'I'm not going to risk being seen with you. Maybe a fast walk will bring you on.'

I looked at him unbelievingly. He couldn't mean to leave me on that dark country road. Could he? He did. Seeing that his words had not sunk in, he gave me a sharp shove.

'I mean it, Marianne. Out you go.'

Without thinking and too shocked to protest further, I did as he said. Then I stood on the grass verge and watched the tail-lights of his car fade into the darkness of that chilly winter evening. Then, still in a daze, I pulled up the collar of my coat and started walking.

When I finally got to our front door his car was already parked next to his front door. I looked numbly at the drawn curtains of his house and pictured him sitting in front of the fire with little thought in his head for me.

I wanted to march up to his door, bang on it, demand he helped, but I knew that he would simply laugh at me and deny any accusations I made. After all, he had got away with it before.

I was on my own and I knew it.

It was nearly two years before he and I spoke again.

Chapter Forty-three

The next few weeks passed in a daze. In the daytime, when I was at the factory, I tried to bury my head in the sand and pushed all thoughts of my pregnancy aside. But in the very early hours of the morning, when terrible and disturbing dreams awoke me, that sinking feeling of dread and fear was already lodged in my churning stomach.

Each time I ran to the toilet to kneel before the bowl as I vomited, I was reminded that too many months had passed for there to be any chance that I was not going to give birth to another child – for, unlike my first pregnancy, morning sickness had not ended after three months.

What was going to happen to me? This was the main question that kept spinning round and round in my head. I tried to will it away as I was just too frightened to contemplate it. I carried on hiding my expanding waist-line under looser clothes, rinsed my mouth with a strong mouth wash to disguise the smell of vomit and burnt matches in the outside toilet to disguise its lingering odours.

It was Bev who noticed first.

'Marianne,' she said quietly at our morning break. 'You're pregnant, aren't you?'

'Yes,' I whispered. Immediately it seemed that just uttering that one word of admission gave me a sense of relief.

She asked me how far gone I was and looked shocked when I told her that I must be in my sixth month. More questions followed, and her horrified expression deepened when I replied that not only had I not been to a doctor but that I had not confided in my parents.

How could I have told her that they would be neither understanding nor supportive? That the reason I knew was that this was the second pregnancy in three years, a fact that I could or would never confide to Bev?

My nails dug into the palms of my hands as I waited for the one question I dreaded more than any other.

'Who's the father?' she asked.

This time I understood what saying I did not know would imply about me. I looked at my feet as I mumbled the prepared lie that it was a boy I had gone out with a few times who had since left the town. 'He buggered off to London,' I embellished. 'Just dumped me after I let him the first time.'

She gave me a sympathetic look. After all, she knew that I had very little social life and I suppose she imagined that I had fallen for the first boy who had shown some interest in me. As I spoke my face flushed, both from embarrassment and also the shame of deceiving my only close friend. Seeing I was very close to tears, she put her arm around me and told me that she would help.

'But Marianne, you have to tell your parents, that's a condition,' she said, and of course I reassured her that I would.

It was Bev who made the doctor's appointment for me and took a day off work to accompany me. The examination confirmed that I was six months pregnant. The doctor made an appointment for me to attend the antenatal clinic and wrote a prescription out for both iron pills and tablets to help stop my persistent morning sickness. I was undernourished, he said, as well as anaemic, and needed good food and rest. He seemed to think that Bev was a relative, for it was to her he addressed most of his comments.

Bev took me home with her afterwards. She fussed over me and made me a cup of tea and opened a packet of chocolate digestives. It was then she told me that she and her husband Phil had talked over my plight.

'We've both agreed,' she said 'that if your parents won't let you stay at home with them whilst you have the baby, you can come to us until everything is over.'

I tried to find the courage to tell my mother but, before I could, matters were taken out of my hands. Three days after my doctor's appointment my father found my medication in my bedroom. When I arrived home from my Saturday-morning shift he was waiting for me.

As soon as I walked through the door my heart lurched as I sensed the strained atmosphere in the room. My mother was standing by the sink as though by looking out of the window above it she was not participating in the drama that was due to unfold.

On the table were the bottles containing my medication, and standing by them was my father. He gave no explanation for the reason he had searched my belongings, and later I wondered just how long he had guessed that I was pregnant. But that day all I felt was fear when he turned on me.

'What are these for?' he asked with deceptive calm.

'They're just iron tablets, Dad,' I replied, and blanched when I saw his face blacken with rage.

In two strides he had crossed the room and grabbed the front of my coat.

'Iron? For what, you little whore?' he yelled. His eyes were blazing with anger that was stronger than I had ever seen before.

'You've fucking well gone and done it again, haven't you?' he shouted, poking me painfully in the chest and stomach with his beefy index finger as he swore at me. As I tried to cover my bump with my hands, his fist, aimed at my stomach, shot out. The air left my body and as I doubled up with the surge of pain I felt his hands grab my limp shoulders. I bit my tongue and my teeth rattled in my head as he shook me.

'What's in there, then?' Eh? You bloody little slut,' and insult after insult rained down on me as, like a rag doll, I was tossed backwards and forwards.

'Who's the father this time? Who's the bleeding father?'

That question that I had been asked so often was now being spewed out of my father's mouth and his spittle flew onto my face. I felt a sudden rage at the unfairness of it. I needed him to stop.

'You know who it is,' I screamed, for I suddenly knew that to be true.

My father shook me again. 'Tell me his name, Marianne,' and I did.

He exploded. 'I knew it! Well, you're not bringing this little fucker home,' and his fist rose to punch me again. Doubled up, still trying to protect my stomach from his blows, I tried to tell him between sobs that I had made arrangements to have the baby elsewhere.

'It's sorted, Dad, it's sorted!' I cried, but he was too far out of control to hear me. Instead he hit me even harder, then threw me across the kitchen table.

One hand held me down whilst the other unbuckled his leather belt. I tried to roll off, tried to crawl away, but my bump made me clumsy and heavy. Down came that belt on my legs, shoulders and arms. I felt the metal buckle slice open my skin, I heard a buzzing in my ears that seemed to mingle with my mother's screams, and then everything went black.

When he finally stopped hitting my limp body he stormed out of the house, telling my mother to make sure I was gone before he returned. As I came round I crawled off the table and went up the stairs on my hands and knees to my bedroom. My stockings were torn, there was blood running down my legs and I was frightened. Frightened that he had harmed my baby.

I sat on my bed, sobbing and hugging my stomach as I tried to get some of my strength back. I kept hoping that my mother would come up and ask if I was all right and put her arms around me and comfort me. But I hoped in vain. Realizing that, I pulled a few clothes and toiletries into a shopping bag and climbed painfully down the stairs using the wall to support my aching body.

My mother was still standing by the sink, but this time her back was against the wall and her hands were over her face. She seemed to have shrunk, and I could see her body was shaking.

'I'm sorry, Mum,' I said. 'I am so, so sorry.'

She did not reply.

'Goodbye, then,' and I waited just for a few seconds for some sort of response. But not receiving it, I walked to the front door and opened it.

It was then that I heard her voice. It was strained and higher pitched than usual.

'Marianne,' she said. 'Look after yourself, love,' and I saw the silent tears raining down her face before I turned and walked away.

Chapter Forty-four

I was oblivious of the pain from my cut leg as I stumbled along the lane to the bus stop. The only thought I held in my head was getting to Bev's house and making sure the beating had not harmed my baby. I felt people staring at me as I clambered onto the bus but I took no notice and just mumbled out the name of the road I wanted to be let out on and handed over the money for my fare to the conductor. I sat at the back of the bus, oblivious to the stares and whispers of the women who kept turning to look at me. I looked out of the window but my eyes were unseeing, for tears blinded them, and I could feel my nose running. In the glass my reflection showed a blotchy face that was already starting to swell.

It was a two-mile walk from where the bus set me down to Bev's house. I could have taken another bus but, as I had always been driven home when I had visited her, I had no idea of where the bus went from. So I just walked numbly down the road.

To my dismay when I reached Bev's house I saw that it was in darkness and remembered too late that this was the evening that she and her husband went out for dinner. My legs buckled and the next thing I remember was the worried voice of Bev's neighbour.

'For goodness' sake, child, whatever's happened to you?' she exclaimed.

She called for her husband, and together they helped me into their front room.

My torn stockings were removed, my cuts were bathed in Dettol and warm water, and my legs were bandaged. All the while she attended to me she kept muttering about me being 'such a tiny scrap of a thing' and that 'someone was going to have to pay for doing this'.

Both she and her husband clearly thought I had been set upon by local hooligans and wanted to call the police, something that I begged them not to do.

They gave me sweet tea for the shock with a drop of brandy in it. I must have fallen asleep on their settee, for the next thing I remember hearing was Bev's voice.

My hand was taken and held tightly and I felt my fingers curl around hers. My eyelids drooped shut again, for all I wanted to do was sleep.

'Marianne,' I heard her say, 'who did this to you?'

'My dad,' I mumbled through swollen lips.

Words like 'bastard' and 'how could he do that his own daughter?' floated in the air above my head as the two women talked about my state.

The women helped me sit up and half carried, half dragged me into Bev's house and up the stairs into her spare bedroom.

The doctor was called and he came out immediately. He examined me carefully and said the baby's heart was still beating. He told Bev and Phil that it was a miracle that I had not gone into an early labour or miscarried.

I heard him mention reporting the incident to the police and then Bev's whispered explanation which included something about my father and, without seeing, I knew his shoulders had shrugged at that bit of information. My father, he knew, would not be the last one that took a strap to his daughter for falling pregnant when underage and unmarried.

Total bed rest was prescribed. 'I'll sign her off work for a week and then we'll see,' he had said sternly to Bev. I heard him leave and then I slept.

I stayed resting at Bev's house for the whole of that week. At the end of it she told me that the personnel manager wanted to see me before I resumed my place on the factory floor.

'Why?' I asked.

'Marianne, come on, you know the rules. The factory doesn't allow pregnant women to work, and there's no way now that they don't know you are.'

She told me then that in fact the older women had known for some time, as had the management, and they had let me work for as long as possible, but it was now time to deal with the problem.

When I went into work that day Bev was right: I was told I had to leave. 'But once everything is over and you've sorted yourself out, there will be a job back here. You are a good little worker,' I was told.

What a funny way of putting it, I mused. 'Once you've given your baby away, they mean,' I thought. My pay and benefits were to be sorted out for me by the personnel department. At lunchtime, much to my surprise, I was presented with an envelope full of money. The workers had taken up a collection for me and, judging by the amount raised, everyone had put in something.

There was enough for me to live on for several weeks, 'not that you have to pay us anything,' Bev said. My tears threatened to overspill at all their kindness.

Two months later, my second daughter was born. This time I gave birth in hospital.

Chapter Forty-five

Bev had looked into the adoption for me, and an agency had been selected. The baby could be taken as soon as she was born, Bev explained to me.

But that suggestion was impossible – I just refused to consider it.

'I can't just hand her over,' I said. 'Even kittens and puppies stay with their mothers until they are weaned!'

'But Marianne, it will make it harder on you,' she tried to tell me as I found more and more reasons to delay the adoption.

I could not admit to her the reason that I already knew that. But still, the thought of handing over my baby without even getting to know her seemed far worse than what I had been through before. At least I still had an image of my first daughter that was fixed in my mind for ever. But if I gave the baby away immediately I would never get to know her.

In the end, when faced with my increasing distress, Bev reluctantly agreed that both the baby and I could stay with them, 'but only for a few weeks,' she stated firmly.

When I went into labour it was Bev, not my mother, who was at my side.

'She's so beautiful,' I said with a sigh, the moment I saw her.

'Yes she is,' Bev agreed.

For those few days that I was in the hospital I felt a contentment. Once again I had a baby, one who fitted into the crook of my arm and lay against my shoulder. The outside world, where decisions had to be made, seemed to become fainter, until I felt that it was just my daughter and me, cocooned in our own little world.

'This one I can't lose,' I thought as I held her tightly against me.

That night I had a dream of the baby and me staying on with Bev and Phil.

After all, she wanted a child, so why could she not have mine? For six weeks, as I fed, held and cuddled my second child, I held fast to that dream. It was Bev who, sensing what was going through my mind, finally made me realize it was simply not going to happen.

She said she and her husband had discussed it.

'Marianne, if we adopted your baby, then we would not be able to see you. It wouldn't just mean that you couldn't stay with us any longer, but then you could not even visit us. Do you understand why?'

I didn't.

I loved her home with its pretty furniture and its clutter. However, this clutter was not like the filth and debris of my parents' home but was confined to magazines laying on coffee tables, and perhaps dancing shoes cast off when they returned home from a night out. Books were in the bookcase, pans and crockery were neatly stacked in the cupboards and the only lingering aroma that clung to the living room was a mixture of cooking, furniture polish and Bev's Yardley perfume.

I also loved that wonderful feeling which I experienced for the first time in my life, of being cared for. Over the months I had known Bev and her husband, I felt she had become, if not a mother figure to me, then a big sister, and the thought of losing her support really frightened me.

She, seeing the conflicting emotions flitting across my face, took my hand as she gently explained why she had reached the decision she had.

'We want our own child,' she explained gently, 'one who only knows me as her mother. But if we adopted yours that would not be possible, would it? You would want to see her if you knew where she was, it's only natural, but that just wouldn't work. It wouldn't be fair to the baby either, being all confused as to who her real mother was.'

I heard her gently explaining to me that my other option, of trying to keep the baby myself, was just not realistic or fair.

When I was sixteen, there was no social security benefit for single mothers or rent-free council flats. An illegitimate child carried a stigma that followed them throughout their lives, whereas I knew the adoption society made sure that 'every baby went to carefully chosen couples who could give them the best upbringing' – words that I had heard before and, deep down, knew to be true.

Bev reassured me that I could stay with them after the baby was adopted. She felt I was still too young and had been through too much to live on my own, and, yes, her husband had agreed to the arrangement.

But there was one condition: I had to put in motion the adoption.

Chapter Forty-six

I hated being in the hospital where happy parents, who I knew would be taking their babies back home, surrounded me. Whereas in the home all the other girls were in the same predicament, here I was the only unmarried mother and certainly the only girl under the age of twenty. So a few days later, as soon as I was ready to, I left the hospital with my baby. Oh, I knew what the pain was going to feel like when I handed her over, but I felt that this time I was more prepared for it emotionally, and having Bev's support might help make it better. I just wanted those few weeks with her, those precious weeks where I could fill the scrapbook in my mind with how she was: her scent, her little cries and the way she looked up at me.

She, like her sister had been, was a good baby. She seldom cried and gurgled with contentment when I bathed her and blew kisses on her body. Her tiny fingers held mine, her eyes looked back at me, and once again I told a child of mine how much I loved her, how I loved her enough to hand her over, so that she could have a better life with new parents who could give her everything.

The day finally came, but this time there was no social worker to talk kindly to me; instead I had ordered a taxi to take me to the adoption agency.

Bev had offered to take the day off work to be with me, but I had said no. However much I was hurting, this was something I was doing for my baby daughter and I wanted to do it alone.

I had bought her a special little dress with puff sleeves and rows of lace going across both the bodice and the hem. Again I wanted the new mother to know that she must have been loved by me. For whereas I knew nothing about the adoptive parents except that they were in a position to offer my daughter the brightest future, they knew my age and a little bit about my background. That alone must have told them why I could not keep her.

Once there, I held my daughter in my arms, breathed in for the last time that special baby smell, then passed her to the woman from the agency.

Her hands came out; I saw on one that the red nail varnish was chipped. It irked me, that flaw, but I don't know why. Then I was aware that it was her holding my baby and that my arms already felt heavy with the loss.

I gave the woman from the agency all the toys and clothes that I had bought and that had been given to me.

'They will buy her everything new,' she said dismissively, but she took them from me anyhow.

'You'll be contacted in the next few weeks,' was all she said after that. 'There are final forms to sign.' Then she whisked my daughter out of the house, down the path into her car and out of my sight.

I went into the kitchen, made a cup of tea, then sat, not drinking it, with my hand resting on that part of me where my bump had been.

This time it was more than pain that I felt, more than numbness and more than loss. It was as though part of me, that part where two babies had lived for nine months, had been scooped out, leaving me hollow and incomplete.

Tears can wait, I told myself, but they didn't.

Chapter Forty-seven

For the next few weeks I was utterly inconsolable. I did not want to eat, get bathed or dressed; I did not even want to get out of bed. When I woke in the mornings my eyes would go to where Kathy's cot had stood beside my bed, only to alight on the now empty space. Throughout the day I listened for her gurgles, only to hear the sound of silence. Each time I forgot, just for a second, that she was not in the room with me I had to cope all over again with the fact that she was gone. I felt a heavy lassitude that weighed down my limbs and dulled my reactions until my whole body ached with the loss I felt for my baby.

I could just not accept that somewhere out there, perhaps only a few miles away, were my two daughters and that I was never going to see them again. All I knew was that I wanted them with me.

I imagined Sonia as she must have been then – a two-year-old, who could already form words and was calling a woman, whom I had never met, Mummy.

Another picture plagued my mind during those days

of intense loss. It was of a woman in a pastel-painted room. I visualized a dimly lit place, where filmy cream curtains moved gently with the light breezes that came from the large picture windows. There was a white wicker cot covered with a soft wool blanket, and by its side there was a pale velvet chair where a woman sat. She was crooning a lullaby to the small form of my youngest daughter, whom she was cradling in her arms.

I looked for my baby's face in that picture, but I never saw it. Instead there was only a blank circle.

It was then, when the pain became too much to bear, that I escaped into my fantasy, one where I had a flat and lived with both of my daughters.

If only, I thought, I could find a job that paid better, then maybe I could get Kathy back. After all, the final forms had not been signed, had they? And until they were, the legal adoption could not go ahead.

Once Bev left for work I would feverishly scan the situations vacant columns in the local papers, ink a ring around the ones that looked promising and then phone them.

Undeterred by the same questions of how old was I, and what work experience did I have, I became used to the responses that followed. They were really looking for someone older – more experienced and with better qualifications. I kept phoning every job where the salary was higher than I had been earning.

I filled a small notebook with my calculations. But no matter how many times I did my sums, when I subtracted the outgoings of a bedsitter's rent and its running costs from my potential incoming wages, there was little left over for food and certainly none for the child care that I would need to provide for my daughters.

Bev left me alone for those first few weeks, but on the sixth one she sat me down and passed over a letter that we both knew had come from the courts.

'You've not signed those final forms, have you?' she asked.

I shook my head guiltily.

'Marianne, you have to let go now,' she said. 'Look, I know I can't begin to understand what you're feeling, but you want your daughter to have the best out of life, don't you?'

'Yes,' I whispered, not wanting to even hear my own answer or to acknowledge that she was right.

'Well, then, sign those forms. I know what you're dreaming of, but, Marianne, it's not going to happen. And think what that other poor woman's going through, the one that has waited for a baby, the one that can give your child everything that you can't. It's not fair to her either to keep her waiting and worrying that you are going to take her baby back. You must know that.'

For the first time since I had known Bev I heard sternness in her voice, as she continued telling me that it was time to leave the world of dreams behind and face reality. I was only sixteen and had my whole life in front of me. I had done the best I could for my baby.

'Marianne,' she added, 'it's brave what you have done. Most girls who have decided on adoption do not even want to see their baby once it is born. But you chose to do it the way you wanted to. But you got attached and made it more difficult for yourself.'

She was right, of course, but even I, who unbeknownst to her, had been through it before, had not known just how hard it was going to be.

'Now,' she added, 'it's time to try and put all of this behind you. I spoke to the personnel officer at the factory. I told her a bit of what you've gone through. She says you're to go and see her as soon as you're ready. She's all set to give you a job doing what you were doing before. So when shall I tell her you're coming?'

'The day after tomorrow,' I eventually said, and she understood from that that I was going to go to the town hall where those papers were waiting for me and finally sign them.

Her voice softened and she took my arm supportively. 'Marianne, do you want me to come with you? I can get a day off if you do.'

Again I said, 'No.' This was the last thing I was going to be able to do for Kathy, and I wanted to do it alone.

That morning I bathed and dressed carefully. I pulled on stockings and the last outfit that Bev had made me before I had grown too large: a circular skirt and crisp white blouse. Now, nearly a year later, it hung loosely on me for I was not only petite but I had lost a great deal of weight since the birth.

Can't be helped, I thought, and I tied a belt around it to camouflage its bagginess. My hair was freshly washed and curled, my make-up was carefully applied and I was ready to take the final step. At sixteen I had just learnt the lesson that make-up and smart clothes can present the image of who we want to be and what we want to feel to those we meet.

It was only a short walk to the bus stop, followed by a few minutes on the bus, but I can remember nothing about the journey. I can only recall closing the door of Bev's house behind me, then being in the town hall. Funnily enough I can remember the click my heels made on the tiled floors as I walked in and I can, in my mind's eye, still see the middle-aged woman in the room my letter told me to report to. She asked me what I had come for.

I told her I was there to sign the adoption forms.

'Oh yes,' was her indifferent reply after I gave my name. Then she fumbled in the drawer of a filing cabinet and passed the forms to me.

'Sign there,' she said in a bored voice as she passed me the pen.

Is that it? I thought as I took it from her outstretched hand. Is that all it takes? Just me facing a disinterested stranger, holding a borrowed cheap plastic pen in my hand and looking at the two places on the form that requested my signature?

I signed that form stating that I was relinquishing all rights to my child, and it all took less than thirty seconds.

Thanks,' the woman behind the desk said as she placed it back in the file. She did not look up again, for her interest in me was so small that it had disappeared the moment the form was back in the file. Without saying another word, I turned and left.

The next day I went to the factory and was given my old job back.

Chapter Forty-eight

I picked up the letter again and stroked it gently with my fingers. When I had first read it just for a few moments, I had wondered if I could still keep my secret, for it was Kathy, my second child, who had written.

'But you deserve the truth,' I thought. 'You have the right to know about your sister, and if you have found me then maybe she will as well. If we meet, the truth must be told.'

That day I talked to my grown-up daughter as if she was sitting next to me on the couch.

'I will not be able to tell you that your father was a boy who disappeared to London, will I?' I said to the empty space. 'You will want his name, where he lived and who he worked for here because you will want to trace him also, won't you? Nor will I be able to say that I don't know who your sister's father was. You simply would not believe me, and anyhow would I want to tell that story to my daughters?' And again I thought of the lie that I had told at thirteen; the lie that had so many repercussions.

As I thought of it my eyes were drawn to the silver-framed photograph on the mantelpiece. It was of my husband and me, taken just a few months earlier. We had been on holiday for a four-day break in the Lake District to celebrate our wedding anniversary.

My husband had arranged it all as a surprise. Then once the arrangements had been made, with a beaming smile he had shown me our tickets for a coach trip plus a four-star hotel. Someone on the same trip had taken the photograph for us, and on my return home I had had it framed.

He, with his height of six foot four, was always so aware that he dwarfed my tiny five-foot frame. His arm was placed lightly around my shoulders, while I looked up at him with a smile wide with love, trust and happiness. As I stared at the photograph and remembered that happy time, another face superimposed itself over my adult one: a face with the soft features of pre-pubescent childhood, one whose eyes looked helplessly back at me. And I saw clearly the child I had once been, a frightened, lonely one – two ingredients that had turned me into a vulnerable child. I shuddered and returned to happier thoughts.

My mind swirled back then to the night when I had met my husband, Bob, the man who had finally made me feel safe.

Since I had returned to work there had been a flood of girls moving down from London to work in the factories. If they had heard any of the stories about me they never mentioned it. Their minds were far too occupied by the latest outfits they wanted to buy and which dancehall was likely to have the best 'talent', as they put it there. A group of them had persuaded me to join their table at the firm's annual dance.

'Come on, Marianne,' said Bev, when she saw me about to refuse. 'Time you started mixing again. Tell you what: I'll make you a new outfit. Got some fab fabric, and made up it will turn a few heads all right.'

With Bev's sewing machine out on the table and yards of pale material spread out, it was almost like old times. Bev cut and pinned, intent on her work. The radio was playing the latest tune and she hummed along although her lips were pursed tightly together holding the spare pins between them. I watched her transform the crisp cotton into something stylish for me to wear.

'Time you had something new and pretty,' she said as she cut out and stitched a square-necked dress that had a tight bodice and a full skirt.

A minibus collected us that evening. It was already half full with girls who were intent on a good night out and were dressed in the newest fashions. As I climbed into it I was suddenly grateful for Bev's input, for I felt my dress looked as good as anyone's there, and suddenly I felt more relaxed. I sat back in my seat and breathed in the atmosphere. The air was heady with a host of different perfumes and, as we got there, there was the 'psst' sound of last-minute hair lacquer being sprayed onto back-combed hairstyles. We were normally a noisy bunch, but with the heightened anticipation of a good night out the noise levels were immense as the girls laughed, cackled and shouted backwards and forwards to each other in light-hearted banter.

As soon as the minibus drew up at its destination our group climbed swiftly out and, clutching our handbags, sauntered through the double doors of the hotel where the function was being held.

A waiter placed a brightly coloured drink in my hand as soon as I arrived and, as I sipped it appreciatively, I found my nervousness decrease.

Following everyone across the foyer, we came into the ballroom where there were long tables laid out for a dinner. At the far end of the room was a large dance floor and a stage where, once we had eaten, a band would play.

It was after the last mouthful of food had been swallowed that one of the new girls leant across the table. 'Hey, Marianne,' she said, 'did you know they've put our names down for the "Princess of the Firm" competition?'

My eyes grew large at that and I looked down the table to where Bev was sitting.

'Don't blame me,' she said laughingly. 'It's the blokes who put your name up – nothing to do with me!'

Another drink was passed my way, and I gulped it down nervously. The thought of walking around that dance floor, with everyone's eyes on me, had the effect of making me want to run to the nearest exit and make a dash for it. I also knew that was not an option. The other eleven girls who had been chosen to take part formed a line, and one grabbed my hand and pulled me up with them.

'Come on, love,' said a pretty blonde girl, 'it's just a bit of fun,' and I watched as she walked the circuit swaying her hips to thunderous applause. Then it was my turn, I walked round that dance floor as fast as I could, hoping my cheeks had not turned that tell-tale pink, and to my utter surprise there were more cheers and claps, this time for me.

The pretty blonde-haired girl won the first prize and I was runner-up. I felt my cheeks turning salmon pink with embarrassment when the ribbon was hung round my neck to even more applause.

Boys came up and asked me to dance and as the band started up I danced with some of the men from work whom I knew.

It was not until the evening was nearly at its end that I noticed a couple of blokes, older than the boys in our group, sitting at a table just watching the dancing. Something really strange happened – a little voice in my head said, 'Ask him to dance.' I did not need the voice to tell me which one of the two it meant – the dark-haired one looked like Simon Templar, the actor who played the lead in the television series *The Saint*.

'No way,' I said to that voice, but it persisted. It was then that I felt as though someone else, a daring adventurous girl I did not know, had taken over my body. For the next thing I knew I was standing in front of them, smiling at the dark-haired one and hearing the words, 'Would you like to dance?' coming out of my mouth.

'You've got a lovely smile,' he said. Then I saw him whisper something to his friend and felt my face go red with embarrassment. I later found out that what he said to his mate was, 'Watch her face when I stand up.'

He looked up at me then and smiled. 'OK, come on then, let's dance,' and as he uncurled himself off the chair I realized I was not much higher than his waist.

'I think you'll have to stand on my toes if all else fails,' he said, and I looked up to find him grinning down at me.

I told him my name and he told me his – Bob.

He asked me how old I was.

'Seventeen,' I replied, and he admitted that he was eight years older.

He took me home that night, and the next day, Sunday afternoon, we went for a drive. I can't remember where we went, but I remember that we just talked and talked, and we got on so well that I felt as though I had known him for ever.

Bev and Phil had been there when he called for me and I knew they were giving him the once over, as they were still very protective of me.

'I'll need to make you some more clothes. You'll need a few changes,' she said with a grin when I got back for tea that first Sunday, 'if you're going to keep going out regularly, that is.'

Whilst we washed up after tea Bev told me she and Phil thought how nice he was. But neither Bev nor I voiced the one worry that that was never far from my mind.

Sooner or later I was going to have to tell Bob about Kathy and I dreaded the thought; it was the only cloud hanging over those early weeks. What would he feel like when he found out about the baby? Every time I saw him my resolve to come clean simply crumbled. I was just so happy being with him that I was terrified of spoiling things. I knew he liked me and he treated me like a delicate flower. What would he say? What would he do?

In the end I swallowed a gin and tonic down in one gulp as we sat in the pub he had driven me to. Before he had even put his pint down on the table I told him that I wanted to talk to him in the car. As a look of concern crossed his face, I explained that I had something I had to tell him.

I had decided to stick to the same story I had given Bev, about the boyfriend who had gone to work in London.

'I know,' Bob said when I had finally summoned up the strength to blurt it all out.

'I've known since the second time I took you out. Blokes talk, you know, Marianne.'

He had also known that I would tell him when I was ready, and he had been waiting patiently for this time to come. He took my tiny hand in his large paw-like one. As he cradled it, he looked into my eyes and talked. Everyone was allowed one mistake. He knew enough about me to know he wanted to marry me. He wanted to look after me. He knew a bit of how my parents had acted when they found out I was pregnant, and he told me that he would never let anyone hurt me again. He said that it was a good thing that the man who had made me pregnant had left town, because if he lived here and if he found out who he was, he just might kill him. After all, I had been under age, hadn't I? An underage and naïve virgin that had been taken advantage of, was how Bob saw me.

But that day the word I heard louder than any of the other words that tumbled from his mouth was 'marry'.

'Marry?' I repeated, perhaps a bit hesitantly for his liking.

'Well, Marianne, maybe I was being a bit big-headed there, but I thought you felt a little for me,' he responded.

I could only stutter out the word 'Yes'. What I meant was, yes I did, and yes, I wanted to marry him.

He wanted me to meet his parents – they would love me, he assured me.

Then he said something I did not want to hear.

He wanted to meet mine.

I went home that night, floating on air. But when I was in bed with the covers pulled up under my chin I heard his words again: 'one mistake'.

That was the beginning of me deciding that the 'one mistake' was all he was ever going to hear about.

Chapter Forty-nine

I knew Bob had heard about my father's bouts of drinking and his temper, but what I was desperately concerned about was what he would think of the home I had come from.

I went to see my mother for the first time since I had been thrown out of the house, carefully choosing a time that my father would be at work.

She told me that she had heard on the grapevine that I was seeing someone and that she was glad for me. I don't know were she got her information from but it was most probably my father. He drank in the same pubs as some of the factory workers.

I told her that Bob knew about Kathy and yet that hadn't stopped him from proposing. I explained that now he wanted to meet them.

'And the other one,' my mother asked. 'Does he know about her, your first baby?'

I shook my head.

'Please, Mum,' I pleaded, 'don't ask me to tell him about that.'

I looked her in the eyes then and held her gaze. 'If he heard about that one, he would want to know who the father was, and he knows me too well to believe that at thirteen I was sleeping around so much that I wouldn't know. And anyhow, I was only thirteen so he'd want that name all right.'

My mother dropped her gaze, sighed and simply told me to bring Bob around on Saturday afternoon.

'Get here before your father has time to go to the pub,' she said.

I wanted to tell Bob about the first baby. I wanted to start married life without any secrets between us, but those words 'one mistake' kept rebounding in my ears. Then something happened that made my mind up for me.

The man from next door appeared at Bev's house. It was on a day that Bev and her husband were at work and I was in on my own.

When I opened the front door I saw a man who for a split second I did not recognize. He was of medium height, more skinny than slight, dressed in clothes that had seen better days – there was a shine to his jacket, a tie with a small tight knot under a frayed collar and his trousers sagged around the knees. Dark hair flecked with grey was slicked straight back, and his eyes added to his general air of seediness as they darted furtively over my shoulder and tried to see into the house. It was his smell that I recognized first: that one of petrol, hair oil and cigarettes.

'Hello, little lady,' he said. 'Aren't you going to ask me in?'

I wanted to slam the door in his face. I wanted him to disappear and I wanted him to be out of my life for ever.

Seeing my wishes clearly written on my face, he put his foot in the doorway and smirked.

'Come on, Marianne, we don't want the neighbours talking, do we? Not when you're so respectable and all. So you'd better let me in, hadn't you?'

I thought of refusing and then I thought of something else; something that might just stop him ever trying to see me again. With my mind racing I took a deep calming breath, then stepped aside.

'What do you want?' I asked as soon as the door was closed, but I knew. Only one thing would have brought him to my door – he wanted what he had always wanted.

But I was no longer a frightened child, was I?

'Hear you're getting married, Marianne. I'm pleased for you. Just thought I would come and give you my congratulations.'

His arms shot out then, trying to embrace me, and I moved quickly to avoid them.

'What's the matter? Haven't you a kiss for your old special friend then? Don't say you've forgotten me already?'

I cringed.

I told him I wanted him to leave the house and that Bev was due back any minute.

'Don't be silly, Marianne, you never were a good liar,' was his reply. 'I know she's working the early morning shift and won't be back till gone twelve.' He looked around the hall, then strode confidently into the sitting room and sat himself down on the settee.

'Only want a little chat,' he said, and I looked at him nervously. His eyes were darting around the room, taking it in. 'Nice comfortable set-up you've got yourself here, isn't it?' I didn't answer him and just waited for him to say what he had come to say.

'So your friend knows about you, does she? Knows about the babies you gave away?' he asked in the same tone of voice that I remembered from my childhood. It reminded me of when he told me he was the only one who could protect me.

'Of course she knows about Kathy,' I snapped. 'I was living here, wasn't I?'

'Wonder what story you gave her, Marianne – surely not the truth?' he replied with another smirk. 'By the way, that little sister of yours is growing up nice.'

I looked at him with loathing then and waves of revulsion mingled with the sudden rage I was starting to feel.

'Bet that big chap you're thinking of marrying doesn't know everything about you,' he said. 'Bet he doesn't know you can't even remember when you were still a virgin.' And as those words left his mouth he knew that they had found their mark and he gave a mocking little laugh.

'Tell you what, Marianne, if you're really nice to me I'll keep quiet about the other one and how old you were.'

His hand rested on the front of his trousers and his face twisted into a predator's leer. It was then that my temper finally swamped any fear of him that I had harboured since I was a child.

'You're wrong there,' I lied, trying to sound as confident as possible. 'My Bob knows, all right. And do you know what he said? He said it made no difference to him, that I was only a child then. Oh, you're right, I did tell him a couple of lies. I said the first one was an older boy at school and the second was someone I had dated. And do you know what Bob said then?'

There was no answer from that seedy little man sitting on the settee. Words seemed to have deserted him, and with a feeling of something approaching triumph I answered my own question.

'He said he didn't want to know their names because if he did he wouldn't be responsible for what he might do, especially to the one who got me pregnant at thirteen. So that's the only secret between Bob and me – your name – and if you know what's good for you it's the one secret you'll appreciate me keeping.'

My whole body was vibrating with rage as I spat those words out and, to my delight, I saw that every word had sunk in – he could tell by my face that he no longer had power over me. 'Oh, and in case you think otherwise I'd better not hear you've got friendly with my sister either – that just might make me remember your name as well.'

He stared at me for a short while and I glared right back, my chin held high. And then, without a word, he got up and walked out. I remember leaning against the front door after he had left, fighting waves of nausea before the realization that I had won finally sunk in.

That was the last time I spoke to the man next door.

Chapter Fifty

I told Bob that I had been to see my mother and that we were welcome to call in the following Saturday. He gave me a warm smile. 'Good for you, Marianne. Now I want you to take Friday off and don't you be booking any overtime this weekend – I've got something special planned.'

'What?' I asked, for I hated being kept in the dark and I didn't want to lose a day's pay unless it was important. But he just gave me a teasing smile and told me I would have to be patient and I'd find out soon enough.

'Just be ready by nine sharp because we're going to London,' was all he would say, and I had to be content with that. Although London was quite close, I rarely went there and I was excited at the prospect.

On Friday morning I was up, dressed and ready for my outing even before Bev and her husband were up.

Something told me that, whatever Bob had planned, it was going to be something special.

We drove part of the way there until we reached an underground station, where we parked the car, then took the tube into London. Rush hour was dying down but I still held Bob's hand tightly as he marched through the crowds. After about an hour and one change of trains, we arrived at Hatton Garden.

'You've never been here before?' Bob asked. Then he laughed when I told him I didn't know where we were.

He took my arm until we reached a small shop. He rang a bell and an old man wearing black clothes opened the door.

'If we are going to meet that dad of yours I think you had better have something to show him, don't you?' Bob said as he ushered me in front of him. The next thing I knew trays of sparkling rings were being placed in front of me.

I was speechless – a ring was something I hadn't given any thought to. Just the fact that Bob wanted to marry me was more than I had dreamt of.

I tried on one after the other; they were all lovely and each one seemed as beautiful as the next. Then my eyes alighted on one that was quite different. It was a simple gold band with a small cluster of diamonds. I slid that one onto my finger, but to my complete disappointment it was too big.

'If that's the one you like, it can be made smaller,' the smiling jeweller assured me, and I felt my face break out in a wide smile when he assured us that it would be ready in an hour.

'Come on, Marianne,' Bob said, 'let's do a bit of sight-seeing and then we can come back and collect it.'

We strolled around the streets and looked at some of the wonderful old churches in the area. I felt as though I was floating on air. We returned on the hour and I tried the ring on for size. It was perfect for my small hand. 'Not yet, you don't,' Bob said laughingly, as he put it back into its velvet-lined box and stowed it securely in his pocket. We found a small cosy Chinese restaurant nearby and sat down to order some lunch. That was when Bob took the ring out of its box and placed it formally on my finger. I felt I would burst with happiness.

'We're going round to my parents this evening,' Bob told me. 'They want to celebrate with us.'

I gulped at the thought of that for I had only met his well-spoken parents once. I thought of the big semi he had grown up in with its comfortable furniture, family photographs, in silver frames on the mantelpiece, water-colours of landscapes hanging on the walls and shelves full of books, and then thought of my parents' home.

As though reading my mind, Bob squeezed my hand. 'It's you I'm marrying, Marianne,' he said, 'and my mother's delighted I'm getting out of her hair and settling down. So stop fretting.'

He was right; his parents greeted us at the door with huge welcoming smiles, and my engagement ring was much admired. Bob's father shook his hand rather formally but his mother reached up on tiptoes and hugged and kissed her son proudly. I was kissed warmly on the cheek and Bob's mother cried a bit whilst his father opened champagne and they toasted us. He made a formal little speech about how pleased they were that I was going to be part of their family.

That night I could hardly sleep for excitement 'Please,' I said, 'if there is a God and you're listening, don't let anything spoil this happiness.'

The next day was Saturday and Bob and I drove to my parents' house for tea. On the drive I twisted the engagement ring nervously round and round on my finger. If Bob noticed, he made no comment; he just kept chatting to me about where we were going to live once we were married. 'Buying is better than renting,' he said and I, happy to agree with whatever he said, just nodded my head.

We reached my parents' house too soon for my liking. I had a sick feeling in the pit of my stomach when I remembered the last time I had seen my father. How was he going to greet us? I wondered what he was going to be like with Bob.

To my surprise it was my father who flung the door open, his hand stretched out to shake Bob's.

'Come on in,' he said, and I realized he had already had a few drinks, enough to put him in a jovial state, but not enough yet to make him turn unpredictable.

'Not going to drink bloody cups of tea when my daughter's honoured us with a visit,' he said, as he brought out bottles of beer for himself and Bob. He then poured two glasses of sweet sherry for my mother and me.

My father said he was happy for us and admired the ring. I knew he would be thinking about what it cost rather than how pretty it was on my finger. My mother showed little emotion and nodded her approval, but I could sense her nervousness.

'Where are my brothers and sister?' I asked, and was told that the elder ones were at their friend's house and the younger one was with Dora.

Suddenly my father looked over at me, and I saw the good humour fade from his face. I braced myself for the inevitable.

'So, Marianne, what have you told your intended about the baby, then?' The room went silent for a second and thoughts of my father telling Bob about both of my daughters flashed into my mind along with the picture of being asked to return my ring. Then Bob spoke calmly but forcefully.

'Look,' he said, 'I want you to get this completely straight. I am not interested in Marianne's past. The only thing that matters to both of us is our future together. She's the woman I love and want to marry and we will do it with or without your blessing. I intend to cherish and take care of her for the rest of my life.'

He stood up then and drew himself up to his full considerable height, crossed to where I was sitting and placed his arm protectively around my shoulders as he looked unsmilingly at my father. 'So you needn't worry about her or,' and here he paused to give his words more impact, 'ever mention that subject again.'

At his words, tears of love and fear formed in my eyes. Oh, my God, I thought, what is Dad going to say now? But my father said nothing, nor in the future did he ever risk Bob's wrath by bringing that subject up again. I turned to Bob, looked up at him and mouthed the words 'Thank you'.

That was the last time my past was ever mentioned.
Eight months later we were married.

Chapter Fifty-one

A few weeks after we had been to Hatton Garden and become officially engaged, Bob told me that he had another surprise for me. He bundled me into his car one afternoon after work and we drove to a road I did not recognize. He pulled up outside a bungalow that had a 'For sale' sign in its front garden.

I looked at him quizzically and he told me that he had put in an offer on it, subject to my approval. Only if I was sure that I wanted this house to be our home would he go ahead and buy it.

'It needs a bit of work, Marianne,' he said, 'but we could do it up at weekends – painting and redecorating together will be fun. I'm not a bad carpenter so I can put in cupboards and a new kitchen too if you like.'

As I walked through the rooms I visualized them painted in light, bright colours with pretty curtains hanging at the windows.

Bev would make those for me, I thought, as I visualized their presence already.

As soon as we had the keys we spent nearly every

evening there working on the house. Bob did the heavy work like sanding down woodwork and I helped him painting walls and scrubbing, then sealing the beautiful wooden floors. We had decided that the bungalow was where our honeymoon was going to be spent and we wanted everything ready for us to move into the day we were married.

Bob told me he disliked hire purchase and insisted that, apart from the mortgage, we didn't want to start married life in debt. As we were going to pay for our wedding ourselves, we decided to get married in a registry office instead of a church.

Bob's parents were a bit disappointed that there was not going to be a big church wedding but they understood that my parents were not in a position to pay for it. They offered to break with tradition, but Bob and I were adamant that we wanted to pay for our own wedding; after all, we were both working. When this was explained to them his mother said laughingly that it was a good thing that she had planted carnation seeds the day we told her we were getting married. She thought they would be ready for us to have as buttonholes on our wedding day!

His father simply said that he knew what he would be doing at weekends, rolling up his sleeves and helping get the house ready for our wedding night.

Flat packs of new furniture were bought and assembled at weekends. New cupboard doors, painted a glossy white, replaced old peeling green ones on the kitchen units, shiny white tiles were laid in the bathroom and Bev's sewing machine worked overtime as matching curtains were made for every room. 'Wedding present,' she said when we thanked her. I was given the task of choosing fabrics and paint for our bedroom. I had told Bob that when I lived at home I had dreamt of having a bedroom to myself. 'So you choose exactly what you want, Marianne. I hope you don't mind sharing the bedroom with me, though!' he said laughingly, and I blushed at the thought of our wedding night.

I had the walls painted a very pale cream, light-blue curtains covered the windows and out of my savings I went to the newly opened Habitat store in London and bought a duvet and a set of blue and yellow covers, pillow-cases and sheets. This would complete our bedroom beautifully, as would the new pine double bed that Bob's parents had given us as a wedding present.

The weeks flew by as we prepared the house. We cele-brated Christmas and then it was time to put the final plans together for the wedding.

Bob's niece and my sister were the bridesmaids, and once again Bev's sewing machine had been hard at work making them blue velvet dresses, trimmed with white fur.

I had already searched the shops for my outfit and finally I found just the thing, a cream knee-length dress and a white fluffy jacket.

Finally, in the middle of February, the big day arrived. I was up at the crack of dawn getting ready. Make-up was carefully applied with Bev's help, and large foam-covered rollers were removed from my hair, which had been care-fully washed the night before. I stepped carefully into my dress and a big white flower was pinned into my hair.

Finally, my feet slipped into white high-heeled shoes, and I was ready.

Bob and I were to travel in the same car to the registry office. 'It's the day we are going to start our journey through life,' he had said to me the night before, 'so we might as well start as we mean to carry on – together.'

When the car arrived Bob got out of it to help me in and I gulped at how handsome he looked with his dark hair sleeked back and his broad shoulders filling out his suit jacket.

I held my posy of tiny white flowers, in a hand that shook with both nerves and excitement, tightly all the way to the registry office. I still could not quite believe that this day had finally come.

My wedding day is now a blur of happy memories – of being so overcome that I could hardly say my own name, friends kissing me and Bob calling me Mrs Marsh.

We left the registry office hand in hand and laughingly half-ran, half-walked through a cloud of confetti to the waiting cars. Bob's parents had booked a restaurant and were taking the entire small group who were at the registry office for lunch.

That day I was pleased to see my parents had made a special effort to look nice. My mother was in a new dress with her hair pinned up, while my father wore a white shirt under a slightly too tight suit jacket.

I can't remember what I ate for that lunch. I can remember champagne being poured, speeches being made and everyone laughing at the best man's jokes. Then it was over and it was back to our house.

Friends had organized a buffet while we had been at the registry office and out for lunch. All I had to do was change and come down to the party, which started as soon as the first person rang the bell. Friend after friend turned up clutching wedding presents of household gifts until there was enough piled up in our spare bedroom to ensure that I had no need to shop for china, saucepans or towels for a long time.

Records were placed on the turntable: Elvis with his latest hit 'It's Now or Never' was followed by new group The Rolling Stones' faster music. As the evening wore on the records changed until Bob and I danced to Frank Sinatra's 'The Last Dance'.

Gradually our friends left until it was just the two of us in our new home. The fire was burning and the new curtains were drawn against the world. As Bob had said, that day was the beginning of our journey together.

Over the years our marriage became a partnership where every decision was a joint one, every holiday was taken together and, when our two sons arrived, childcare was shared. It was a perfect marriage, a marriage built on trust; only marred for me by the secret that I carried for so many years. Every Christmas when I looked at the happy faces of my two sons I remembered that other one when a group of girls had sat with their babies trying to pretend they were part of a family.

Oh, so many times I had wanted to tell Bob, but I never found the courage to admit that it hadn't only been one mistake.

'And now you've written,' I said to the invisible presence of my daughter.

When the law changed, allowing adopted children to trace their birth parents once they turned eighteen, I knew that this day might come. And, as I whispered those thoughts in the empty living room, I knew that I had reached the day when the decision about what I was going to do could no longer be put off. I thought of the happy years of marriage that lay behind me. I pictured our two sons, grown men now, who, like their father, stood at well over six feet.

I thought then that it was not just my husband I had deceived all those years but both of them as well.

Chapter Fifty-two

I picked up another envelope from the coffee table. Inside were two letters that I had never posted. I had written them at the time when that adoption law had changed.

In them I told each of my daughters in turn how much I had loved them and how I had never forgotten them or ceased to miss them.

'And if one day you decide to find me,' I had written, 'will you bring all those photographs that tell the story of the years I've missed – those pictures taken of you as a baby and then as a toddler, when you were just learning to walk? I want to know how you looked on your first day at school, read one of your reports to see if you have any of my interests. Your parents, the ones you have called Mum and Dad, will have those memories imprinted in their minds, whereas mine stop when you were just a few weeks old. They can look at them, those memories of all the magic moments, at will, smile at some and chuckle at others. And I just want to borrow them, to pretend for a short time that they were mine.'

The hours ticked by without me noticing that the day was passing. It was not until I heard the door open that I realized it was late afternoon. I heard my husband's voice calling out to me, and then he was in the room.

'Marianne, whatever is the matter?' he asked the moment he saw me huddled on the settee, and it was when I heard the note of concern in his voice that I broke down. Tears of guilt and shame poured down my face.

I passed him the letters I had written.

'Read them,' I said.

For a few minutes, apart from the rustle of paper, there was silence.

'You had two daughters,' he said. 'Two, not one?'

His voice, I realized then, was more sad then angry. But still I was unable to look at him.

'Thirteen!' he said incredulously. 'You were thirteen and you went through that? Why did you never tell me?'

I told him I had been too ashamed, that I had felt that way about myself since I was eight. Then for the first time in my life I blurted out the whole story of my childhood and the man next door. As I spoke, I could feel Bob's anger filling the room and I shrank into the corner of the settee.

He asked me questions, until finally the whole story was out.

'The bastard, the bloody bastard,' he said, when he learnt that the man next door had fathered both my children.

'Maybe you were right not to tell me,' he said, at last, 'because if I had known I don't know what I might have done to that bastard.'

Gradually he reassured me that his anger was only for what had happened to me.

He was just so sorry, sorry that I had carried that burden for so long.

'Marianne,' he said at last, as he watched me sobbing for the past and for the future, 'listen to me! You did nothing wrong. You were only a child. Oh, you might have known what was happening was wrong, but you could not have understood why. Children don't. God, you must have been so frightened, so unhappy! And your parents did nothing to stop it! Your father is such a bully. If it were my daughter, I'd have killed him. I swear it.'

It was then that I showed him the letter from my daughter.

We talked for the rest of that evening. I asked what our sons would think.

'Things have changed since we were young, Marianne,' was Bob's answer to that. 'You're their mother, and they love you as much as I do. Nothing is going to change that. We'll invite them up this weekend and tell them together.' He kissed me then, and as I felt the warmth of his body and of his spirit I felt safe again.

'So, I guess you have rather a special phone call to make in the morning.'

Epilogue

I would like to say that a week later, when I opened the door to my daughter and my grandchild, if we had met somewhere else we would have instantly recognized each other. That the bond I had felt all those years ago had somehow kept us connected. But I can't. I simply saw an attractive young woman standing on the threshold.

And was I the person she had imagined? I asked this of her after we had talked for a while. 'No,' she had replied, 'because I have always thought of you as that vulnerable fifteen-year-old girl who had been made to give her baby up for adoption.'

We talked, my daughter and I, of the years that had passed, and she showed me the photographs that when I made the telephone call I had asked her to bring.

I was wrong about them, and as one by one I looked at them I realized that there was no substitute for shared memories – they were just pictures of a child I could not recognize.

I told her that she had a sister and finally explained who her father was.

She took it in her stride, for after all the man who had brought her up was her real father, as was his wife her real mother. It hurt to hear that, but I am glad she felt that way; it meant they had loved her, they had made her their own and she had been happy.

When they left, with her promises to keep in touch, I cried for what was my irrevocable loss.

Bob and I told our sons together that they had two sisters. Their response was to ask when they were going to meet them.

Sonia, as I had hoped she would, traced and contacted me a year later.

She was overjoyed to learn she had a sister and a niece, and their meeting was a happy one.

She had never married, she told me; maybe it was her adoptive parents' cold marriage that had put her off that idea.

Sadly I learnt that my eldest daughter had never connected with the couple that had adopted her. They were middle aged when she went to them and she told me that it was a house without laughter.

I felt, as I remembered that tiny baby dressed in that boy's blue romper suit, that she blamed me for that. Or maybe this was just the guilt I felt, for I had wanted at least to hear that both my daughters had been happy.

Since we met Kathy, whose name her adoptive parents never changed, her family has increased and I am a grandmother several times over. We keep in touch with birthday and Christmas cards and even the occasional visit.

Sonia decided that, whereas she wanted to stay in touch with her sister, there was too little to connect us to warrant staying in contact. I still hope one day she will change her mind.

When Bob sees that look on my face, the one that tells him my mind has slipped back to my teenage years, he takes my hand and tells me that not every memory can be a happy one. 'But,' he says then, 'I'll try and make the new ones good.'

And he does.

what's next?

Tell us the name of an author you love

| Marianne Marsh | Go ▶ |

and we'll find your next great book